ON INDIA'S FRONTIER.

ON INDIA'S FRONTIER;

OR

NEPAL

THE GURKHAS' MYSTERIOUS LAND.

BY

HENRY BALLANTINE, M. A.

GYAN

Published by

Gyan Publishing House
5, Ansari Road
Daryaganj, New Delhi-110002
Phone: 011-47034999, 9811692060
E-mail: books@gyanbooks.com

Distribution Network
gyanbooks.com
India, USA, Canada, UK, Australia, France

ISBN: 978-81-212-7975-8 (PB)
First Published, 1895

2nd Impression 2023

Printed at: Gyan Press, Delhi.

ON INDIA'S FRONTIER
Author: HENRY BALLANTINE

ON INDIA'S FRONTIER.

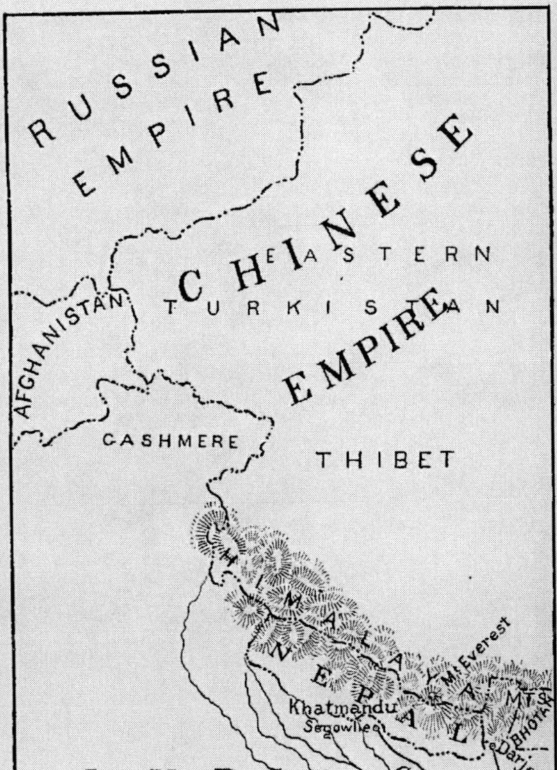

RUSSIAN EMPIRE
CHINESE EMPIRE
EASTERN TURKISTAN
AFGHANISTAN
CASHMERE
THIBET
HIMALAYA MTS.
Mt Everest
NEPAL
BHOTAN
Khatmandu
Segowlie
Darjeeling
INDIA
HINDOSTAN
GANGES RIV.
CALCUTTA
Bay of Bengal
Scale 350 Miles to inch.
Mr Ballantine's route

ON INDIA'S FRONTIER;

OR

NEPAL

THE GURKHAS' MYSTERIOUS LAND.

BY

HENRY BALLANTINE, M.A.

LATE AMERICAN CONSUL AT BOMBAY. AUTHOR OF "MIDNIGHT MARCHES THROUGH PERSIA."

NEW YORK

J. SELWIN TAIT AND SONS

65 FIFTH AVENUE

To

HONORABLE CHARLES P. DALY,

FOR OVER A QUARTER OF A CENTURY

President of the American Geographical Societ

AND ONE OF THE FOREMOST PROMOTERS
OF GEOGRAPHICAL RESEARCH,

This Volume is Respectfully Dedicated

BY

THE AUTHOR.

ON INDIA'S FRONTIER;

OR

NEPAL, THE GURKHAS' MYSTERIOUS LAND.

By HENRY BALLANTINE, M. A.

Late U. S. Consul to Bombay.

INTRODUCTION.

"Hitherto shalt thou come, but no further" may be said to be the dictum of the British Foreign office, written and expressed all along the northern boundary of India's frontier, and he "may run that readeth it." The traveler must abide by this ruling, especially if he be a Feringhi, or white man, anywhere within the borders of British India, whether he be English, American, German, French, or of any other foreign extraction, contemplating the passage of this boundary with a motive ever so peaceful, friendly, or disinterested.

He who would overstep this political demarcation from any point on the Hindustan side, is at once seized, brought back into India, and ordered to return whence he came.

As long ago as Sir John Lawrence's time, and since then more zealously and jealously maintained, there has been mapped out by England, under the supervision of the India Government, a Neutral Belt, with the Himalaya Mountains for its southern base, and extending up northwardly, comprising vast stretches of little known, and most of it quite unknown, territory, divided up among independent tribes more or less hostile to each other. These tribes are furnished with arms and ammunition, in certain cases to a large extent, by the India Government, and are left to act as they please, so long as they do not meddle with British territory. They constitute what are known as the "Buffer" States and are used, one and all, as a breakwater against the ever-threatening flood of Russian invasion from the far north.

Whenever there is the slightest indication of what may seem like Russian aggression towards this British-constituted belt, it is deemed a sufficient signal of alarm for the

India Government to do its utmost to head off Russia's apparent attempt to invade India, or to call upon that Power for an explanation, or enter upon a rearrangement of the boundaries of the so-called Neutral Belt, encouraging the tribes within its borders by bribery, or self-interest even, to maintain it intact. Any apparent encroachment upon this boundary is tantamount to a *casus belli.*

From the foregoing it will be seen that the Policy of the India Government is to let the northern frontier tribes maintain their independence, continue to practice deeds of darkness and misrule, allow them to cherish any internecine course of action they like, while, as the paramount power, this Anglo-Indian ruler retains the right to interfere, as may best suit its purposes, even to the extent of taking the part of the stronger against the weaker side, and freely distributing war material to those whom it favors;—anything, in fact, that will promote its frontier policy.

On the other hand, great as England has proved herself to be as a general ameliorator of those subject, even at a distance, to her dominant sway, it cannot but be regretted that her representatives in the far East should persistently discourage any commercial, enlightening, or civilizing attempts from outside to reach the natives inhabiting this particular belt, who so long as they act as able guards and protective outposts, ranging themselves into a bulwark of resistance against northern intrigue, so long have they their independence assured them, and their harmful exclusiveness guaranteed and abetted by this same India Government.

We are constrained at this point to go back and pay tribute to those grand types of men who laid the foundations of the present great Empire of India.

There were giants in those days, in every sense of the word, men of unflinching principle and of great capabilities, unswayed by partisan interests or political sympathies, commissioned and sent out under the auspices of the famous, liberal, The Honorable East India Company. These officials can never be equalled by their present successors in the East; while their example and good works stand out beyond all comparison, and beyond any possible competition by the present race of Lilliputians, stigmatized competition-wallahs—(those selected by competitive examination), who compose the Anglo-India rule of to-day; at the same time I have no doubt that if similar desperate emergencies should arise British valor and splendid capabilities would not be found wanting.

Those were times too when men were trusted to do their best by the far off country they represented, and to the country to which they were accredited and governed; inasmuch as they, being on the spot, were naturally, and wisely supposed to act according to the needs of the hour and the sudden requirements of their peculiarly strange surroundings, instead of being dictated to and hampered from a distance of 8,000 miles, as in the case of the present officials; and that too by men in London who have never lived in India,—some not even having seen the country,—and who, in consequence, despite cablegrams and rapid steam communication, can never comprehend the situation, or realize the nice adjustments requisite for meeting and harmonizing so many conflicting elements as are crowded into their Eastern Empire with its 300,000,000 inhabitants of diverse creeds and languages, and kept in order by 60,000 British soldiers, assisted by twice that number of sepoys or native troops

Nepal, the subject of these pages, the mountainous home of a recklessly brave and hardy race known as the Gurkhas, ranks as the most powerful and favored of India's frontier tribes.

Outside of a small, select British official class, who have been posted there at different times by the India Government to watch after its interests, the number of other foreigners permitted to visit Nepal can be counted on one's fingers, and these during their short licensed sojourn in that territory are under constant espionage. No wonder, then, that Nepal is a *terra incognita*—an unknown as well as a mysterious land—to the outside world. Though nominally subservient to China, paying its tribute quintennially to the Celestial

Empire, it virtually recognizes the direct supremacy of Great Britain, to which power first and foremost, in the personnel of its foreign office, application must be made for any permission to enter this country's borders, declaring in detail the plan and object of the applicant's projected trip, with all particulars concerning himself; and, even then, his request is likely to be denied.

Hence the title of this little work—

"ON INDIA'S FRONTIER,
OR NEPAL, THE GURKHAS' MYSTERIOUS LAND."

ON INDIA'S FRONTIER;

OR NEPAL, THE GURKHAS' MYSTERIOUS LAND.

CHAPTER I.

PREPARATIONS FOR THE START.

"Travel has lost all romance" was a remark made by a Russian officer to the writer as we were ascending the Volga in a magnificent steamboat built after the most approved American model. This sentiment was reiterated afterwards in the United States by an American under very different circumstances, and again expressed by a British officer when steaming down the Red Sea, as a fellow passenger, on board one of the Peninsular and Oriental Company's boats bound for Bombay.

Something of this idea is expressed by the orthodox Mahomedan and Hindoo, whose conception of romance, if any, is somewhat vague and tinged with a religious sentiment. This is especially the case when they begin to question the merit of a pilgrimage, the one to holy Mecca, the other to sin-emancipating Benares, borne on the flight of steam and under the patronizing guidance of the ubiquitous Cook and Son. On that account both contrast these times unfavorably with the good old meritorious days of their fathers, when there were no facilities for travelling, and when it was as rare as it was difficult to become a venerated Hāji, or a revered pilgrim from Kasi (Hindoo for sacred Benares).

However, all this concerns us not. We have a story to tell, a simple unvarnished tale, and our readers must decide whether all travel is destitute of romance, and if there should be any Hindoos among the number we would seriously inquire of them from *their* point of view whether we cannot lay claim to some *punya* or merit—"Treasure in heaven."

Since every story, as well as every journey, must have a beginning, we will start from Darjeeling, and commence by asking the reader where this is. Even presuming that he knows

DARJEELING—7,000 FT.
(Through the Morning Mists.)

all about the place, we will be presumptuous still, and state that Darjeeling is a sanitarium, a city on the Himalaya Mountains, 7,000 feet above sea level, 375 miles due north of Calcutta, and brought within twenty-four hours of that city by direct railway communication.

It is surrounded by tea gardens, whose products have already outrivalled those of China, and is as great a resort as it is a boon to worn-out Calcuttaites and other people of India's plains.

The climate is bracing, and the scenery grand, the most prominent feature of the landscape being Mt. Kinchenjunga, 43 miles distant in a straight line, across deep valleys and precipitous ranges, piercing the sky with its quadruple head, scarred with age and white with driven snow, 28,000 feet above sea level. It is the second highest point of land in the world. From Darjeeling one can look off and over into Nepal and upon the mountains of Bhootan, Sikkim and Thibet.

The writer and his son, Harry, a lad of thirteen, wished to visit Nepal, a country probably unknown to most readers. It embraces a stretch of territory 500 miles long by 150 wide, named after the defunct and venerated Hindoo Saint the ascetic Ne.

It starts from the Terai (a low, flat, heavily timbered land that skirts the base of the Himalayas, teeming with wild beasts, and as hot as it is malarious), extends upwards over the Himalayan ranges in front, and stretches onward till stopped by such hoary sentinels of the north as Mts. Everest, Yassa and Diwalgiri. Such is the situation of Nepal, embracing all the climates of the world, but averse to include in this embrace any foreigner like the European, against whom particularly it fosters a jealous antipathy.

How then were we to enter Nepal? It is true we could walk out of our Darjeeling house in a westerly direction along a moss-carpeted, tree-lined road, skirting precipices overlooking tea planters' cottages, and their tea gardens, and in four or five hours come upon certain white masonry pillars that mark the line between British and Nepalese territory. Passing these we should be on Nepalese soil; but this is not what we meant by visiting Nepal.

KINCHENJUNGA—28,156 FT.
(Through Storm Clouds from Darjeeling.)

We use the word Nepal here in the sense the native does. When he speaks of going to Nepal, or coming from there, he means Khatmandu, the capital of the Gurkha dynasty, in Lat. 27° 42′ N. and Long. 85° 36′ E.; fully 26 days' march by slow difficult stages from Darjeeling.

This route, however, was quite out of the question, as no European is permitted to enter from this direction. Aware of this we applied first to the British Resident for the requisite pass. This official is a sort of consular officer appointed by the British Government to represent it at Khatmandu. He promptly replied, discouraging our coming, but offering to send a permit if we persisted in our wishes. We wrote again and got the necessary document both in the English and vernacular, giving us the desired permission, although the Resident again strongly discouraged our coming, representing it to be a very difficult undertaking, and urging us to give up the adventurous project. This we did not feel inclined to do, even though the route detailed to us was in confirmation of the old adage that "the longest way around is the shortest way home."

CHAPTER II.

FROM DARJEELING TO SEGOWLI.

Accordingly, one sharp frosty morning, with Kinchenjunga reflecting the beams of a brilliant sun, we took seats on board a miniature train on a two-foot gauge railway—a twelve-ton engine attached to a dozen trolleys or hand-cars—and after passing down gradients of 1 foot in 28, into loops, figure 8's, zigzags and curves (the sharpest being of 70 feet radius), over foaming torrents, and through moss-festooned forests, all along catching most magnificent panoramic glimpses, we had descended by evening some 7,000 feet in 48 miles, and reached the dead level of the Gangetic plain.

Here we boarded something more like a railway train, and reached Calcutta by noon the following day.

A simple reference to the map will show

HIMALAYAN RAILWAY TRAIN.
(Ascending to Darjeeling.)

VICEROY'S PALACE AND PUBLIC BUILDINGS—CALCUTTA.

that this was going right away from Nepal, but combining, as it did, railway facilities with the most feasible route over the Himalaya ranges, it was our best and quickest way. In Calcutta we laid in a stock of provisions put up in tin, such as biscuits, butter, jams and meats, and, under this last named head, the pressed corn beef of Chicago or St. Louis deserves to be recommended as *par excellence*, the best for a rough jungle life. Besides, we provided ourselves with a set of cooking utensils of light block-tin ware, and also a few dishes, and engaged a Nepalese servant for cooking and general usefulness, although it would have been difficult to find a man who would have better filled the bill for slovenliness, shirking his work, and general inefficiency.

The last night of October found us well loaded down in a ticca-gharry—the wretched but useful public horse conveyance of Calcutta. We drove through the city down to the river Hugli* and across the much-used

* The lower portion of the river Ganges and its main outlet into the Bay of Bengal is called the Hugli, often spelled Hoogly.

floating bridge, the only one this proud metropolis can boast of at present, over this sacred branch of the Ganges. On the other side was the Howrah Railway Station, a very poor building that serves as the terminus of such an important artery as the East India Railway, owned and operated by the Government of India.

The usual buying of tickets, weighing and paying for luggage—an extortionate form of business—and getting it properly labelled, being safely concluded, during which red-tape process, the "booking-clerk," a West Indian of the color of midnight, had the satisfaction of informing me that he bore the same unusual name as mine, and therefore must be related to me. All this and the paying off of coolies having been successfully accomplished, with my son and servant I got comfortably arranged for the night, when the train started punctually at nine o'clock, averaging a speed of thirty miles an hour including stoppages.

At seven o'clock the next morning we steamed into the station of Mokameh, some 300 miles from Calcutta, and changed from

THE HUGLI AT CALCUTTA.

the standard broad-gauge railway to the narrower one of the Tirhoot State Railway; though, as a preliminary, we had to cross the Ganges, by a well appointed steam ferry—rather an awkward operation if undertaken in a dark, rainy night when the precipitous character of the muddy bank is taken into account.

All day we travelled at the modest speed of 13 miles an hour, due north, through a most fertile, well-populated country, flat as a billiard table, and through a district which has long been noted for its indigo plantations, owned and managed by some of England's best blood; sons of gentlemen and retired officials about whom it can certainly be said from our own experience, that their hospitality is most generously dispensed to any white man travelling in their midst.

At 6 P. M. weary and travel-stained we arrived at the little station of Segowli, situated in the territory of the Maharaja of Bettiah. Here we were bundled out hastily bag and baggage upon the platform, the train being behind time and only a minute allowed for stopping.

We rubbed our eyes, counted our packages, about twenty large and small, managed to get a sufficient number of coolies together to carry them, and trudged along for more than a mile in the dark to a "Travellers' Bungalow," or rest-house, belonging especially to the engineering department, who had charge of that section of the great macadam road built through Tirhoot.

The Bungalow, on being opened by the man in charge, we found to contain some chairs, a table or two, and above all a couple of easy beds. These last we eyed with no small degree of comfort and immediately patronized, hardly allowing time for ourselves to dispatch a simple supper hurriedly prepared by our Nepalese servant.

CHAPTER III.

TROUBLE IN SECURING COOLIES.

We rose the next morning, but somewhat after the sun, and at once set to work to make arrangements (the expressive native term "*bundobust*" well describes this) for the transport of ourselves and effects over the 96 miles that lay between us and the Nepal capital Khatmandu, or at least that first portion of it traversed by a cart road.

We began by trying to procure coolies who would march clear through at the Government stipulated rate of four and one quarter rupees, or about seven shillings each man; but this attempt failed, as only half a dozen coolies were available. We then, after much trouble and delay, managed to secure a bullock cart, the ordinary common conveyance of India on two wheels and drawn by a couple of bullocks. Upon this we loaded our luggage and in the evening sent it ahead by our Nepalese servant.

For ourselves we planned to hire two ponies, as we had brought saddles, but no ponies were to be had. Then we thought of walking rather than be delayed another day. However, at the last moment, an ekka was procured for us, the driver of which bound himself by agreement (and confirmed the same according to native custom by taking an advance of two rupees) to carry us to Bechiakoh, forty miles distant, where the road-way terminates.

I must explain to some of my readers that an ekka is a small two-wheeled, springless conveyance with a sort of bell-shaped top to screen its occupants from the sun, drawn by a single pony, fastened within a pair of bow-shaped shafts, resting on a high padded wood saddle bound on his back, the whole rig being dubbed by many a "Jingling Johnny."

The vehicle can accomodate fairly one passenger, besides the driver who straddles the shafts, seated *a-la-Turk*, with a few bits of baggage stowed away in a sort of cage or netting about the axle.

EKKA—INDIA'S ONE HORSE CONVEYANCE.

This gig or "rig" is very common throughout northern India, and drawn as it is by a single hardy brute of a pony, one can travel by it at a dog-trot all day long, making often astonishing distances in a few hours. The writer has been carried 60 miles in an ekka drawn by the same animal between sunrise and sunset, and he has known of one making 150 miles inside of two consecutive days.

Night having now set in (with occasional dashes of rain to aggravate our situation) the owner of the ekka proposed that he be allowed to go to his house near by so as to feed his pony well, promising that he would be back again soon, ready to start anytime after midnight. We fell in with this plan as it admitted of our indulging in a little sleep and getting some rest before starting. after the strain of the previous day.

For some reason the pony and his driver did not appear until towards morning, and we too were loath to rise and face the untried day. However, by 4 A. M. Harry and I were up, when it was the work of a few minutes only to arrange ourselves in the ekka and be off.

Our progress at first was very slow and painful, as it was still dark and the road very rough, cut into deep ruts and pitfalls, that were regular bone breakers—the results of the now closing monsoon—while a heavy fog enveloped everything, rendering the night air chilly and penetrating.

With the dawning of the day we got along better, and by 8 o'clock had made about twelve miles. Here at the little village of Rugganathpore we procured some rich buffaloes' milk, and with the help of a tin of biscuits made out a very fair "chota-hazri," or the simple early morning repast of "tea and toast" common in the east.

We caught up with our bullock cart and servant at this place, though they had the start of one night before us. Such slow progress was not much to their credit, and we accused them of having halted during the night somewhere. This of course they denied. As our pony had shown signs of giving out, I told the driver that he must not take him on any further, but must get another in his place.

At first he refused to comply, but I insisted and finally he made a change by getting another pony from an acquaintance in the village. I had some reason to be sorry for having interfered at all in the matter, for the new brute turned out to be a wretched affair, and would in any museum have required a label to denote his species.

We made this a pretext for asking the driver to run beside the ekka and not sit in it. This gave us more room, and lightened our load by half, for the man was a large heavily built fellow, weighing as much as both of us together.

CHAPTER IV.

DESERTED BY HORSEMAN AND CARTDRIVER.

With the driver running alongside for some six miles we reached Ruksoul, the end of British territory and beginning of Nepal—the boundary line being a small treacherous looking stream with precipitous muddy banks and bad crossing. We found it readily fordable, but in the monsoon it must prove dangerous to travellers, if not positively impassable—a place above all others for a bridge, which need not be an expensive affair either, judging from the logs lying about, brought from the neighboring forests of the Terai, that so-called extensive wooded belt of land already alluded to as skirting the base of the Himalaya mountains.

All along the way thus far we had been straining our eyes to catch a glimpse of the famous towering ranges of Nepal often plainly seen from Segowli, but there was nothing now visible save one monotonous stretch of dead level land, covered with newly sown crops of rice, wheat and pulse. Still we knew that the mountains were near, and that we could have seen them but for the murky atmosphere.

The noonday sun began now to beat down fiercely, causing intense radiation and distorting objects all along the line of vision, while the heat itself was almost prostrating. Suddenly our bad road grew worse and soon became no road at all.

This gave a pretext to the driver to declare that both he and his pony were thoroughly exhausted, and that to go on was out of the question. Of course we would not allow for a moment any such complete giving out, particularly as we had ourselves taken to our legs with the determination of doing our utmost to reach Persowny for the night. I must confess that it did seem as though we should never reach this town, as we trudged on past fields, mango groves, and villages, although it is reckoned only twenty-six miles from our early morning starting point of Segowli.

At length by 3 o'clock in the afternoon, we were rewarded by the sight of the mud walls and houses of the town which proved to be a good-sized place, and was holding at the time one of those large, well attended weekly bazars so common in India.

After much questioning, searching and a trial of patience, we secured shelter in the large garden of a Guruji (Hindoo Priest), under cover of a thatched roof open on all four sides.

At first we were beset by a very inquisitive crowd, but with management we got rid of them without hurting anybody's feelings, and I must say that we secured every attention from the persons in charge of the garden, one of whom was a Brahmin who thought he spoke good English, and offered his services as guide for our journey, which services, however, we respectfully declined. He got us a "healthy chicken," his way of describing one in good condition, and some "wealthy milk!"

A couple of hours after our arrival our cart came along, and we were glad to get out our things so as to make ourselves comfortable, and set our man to cooking a breakfast, dinner and supper all in one.

The ekkawalla—our driver—now presented himself and declared he would not go on any further, and asked to be paid off. We reminded him of his agreement and asked how he supposed we were going to manage if he left. This did not concern him, but return he must, as the road was simply impassable, endangering his ekka and pony, with a lot of more nonsense to the same effect. Then too he wanted more money which was really the secret of his aversion to proceeding.

I had, however, already over-paid him and positively declined to let him have any more, or give my consent to his returning. He then assumed an impertinent tone and began talking insolently, threatening to leave anyway. He also got hold of the cart man and incited him to demanding his discharge and the less notice we took of him or his threats, the more boisterous and offensive he became, thinking that now, as we were hard pressed, he could force us to submit to all of his extortionate demands.

For a native I am bound to say he was an exceptionably "bad lot," just the kind that now-a-days hang about the centres of European travel, where alone they seem to thrive, fattening on the white man's weaknesses; encouraged if not actually protected in their nefarious practices all over British territory by a large class of magistrates and the laws in which they are steeped, although I am more disposed to find fault with the latter than the former.

What the man really deserved was a good horse-whipping (it would have converted him as no court proceeding could) and had he still persisted, our feeling of silent contempt for the wretch might have given place to some decisive and more effective action. However, just at this moment our servant announced that the soup, nice chicken curry, etc., were ready; and being famished, no distraction or insolence, not even the gaping inquisitiveness of a few uninvited onlookers could keep us from first satisfying the demands of hunger.

This proved a good opportunity for the ekka driver and cartman to slip away quietly with all their belongings, leaving us to make shift as best we could. Such a predicament was hardly a desirable situation, but after all it was hardly unexpected, for one who would travel in India successfully must not be surprised at, or unprepared for, the worst exhibitions of human character and cunning. Having already had many years of this edifying process of schooling, we accepted our situation as a matter of course and laid ourselves down to undisturbed sleep, the last thing I was conscious of being the gradual fading away of the brilliant constellations, Orion and the Great Bear, as their twinkling rays struggled through our drowsy eyelids and invited us to sounder slumber, all the while caring naught for pariah dogs that snapped and snarled over the fragments of our supper almost within reach of my feet, nor for jackal scavengers that screeched and hooted at their lagging companions in the adjoining hedges.

CHAPTER V.

THE TERAI FOREST.

The morning sun well up above the horizon was the first to rouse us, shining full in our faces, and bidding us be up and off. But how were we to go without even a cart to carry our luggage? The town was at once ransacked for some sort of conveyance, and by offering prepayment of the entire sum asked, not a wise course to adopt ordinarily, but now absolutely necessary, especially as the price asked was not exorbitant, we secured a bullock cart for our effects.

While this was being loaded the favorable report got about of our being good payers. At once two ponies were brought for us to ride. We hardly expected this, having made up our minds that we were to walk the rest of the way, a course much to be preferred to riding the wretched animals one usually finds for hire on such an out-of-the-way journey.

The weather, however, was abnormally warm for the season of the year, making any special physical effort more of a task than a pleasure; so we were not loath to put on the saddles, mount the fragile creatures and accompany the cart.

There was no danger of our getting ahead (we tried and failed) for these four-footed specimens did not know any gait beyond a walk. But we found one thing to console us in our slow progress; as soon as we got clear of the outskirts of Persowny and its surrounding clumps of bamboo, tamarind and mango trees, a magnificent stretch of forest-covered mountains burst upon our sight.

The scene was charming and a great relief to the monotonous, flat, highly cultivated plain we had been traversing almost the whole way from Calcutta, and which within a distance of eight miles as we looked ahead, seemed to be brought to a very abrupt termination in a dark, deep, well-defined border running east and west, extending beyond all possible range of sight, apparently thrown around this monstrous growth of a plain to stop its repacious greed.

This border consisted of a wild; malarious uninhabited jungle called the Terai forest proper, some ten miles wide, opposite the point where we were to enter it, and extending over a thousand miles, right across the whole of upper India, and as if such a belt should not prove a sufficient barrier to check the encroachment of the plain, there arose on the outer side of the belt, quite as abruptly as the latter did out of the plain itself, range upon range and tier after tier of the most stupendous chain of mountains, each overtopping the other, till they ended in the eternal snows and the everlasting blue of heaven.

Wrapt in admiration of this enchanting prospect we gave no further thought to our slow progress, or to the snail's pace at which our wretched ponies crept along with us.

By one o'clock, under a blistering sun, we reached the Powah or Rest-house, something like a Persian Caravansery, of the dirty little village of Semrabassa, where we put up in the open veranda, it being the cleanest place.

We had traveled only ten miles since morning and would have liked to have had a much greater advance to show for our day's march. We had come right up to the edge of the Terai forest, which like a dark, ill-omened barrier, sharply silhouetted against the mountain background, stretched directly across our pathway, and from one horizon to another. We were, however, strongly advised not to attempt penetrating its forbidding-looking gloom and its weird shadows that afternoon.

So, with no alternative but to acquiesce in our situation, we set about making ourselves as comfortable as possible, and had the benefit of watching our servant prepare our dinner—a very unwise thing to do, and which certainly did not tend to give us an increased relish for our food.

By dark, dinner being over, we were ready to retire, but little sleep could we get, as the night was Dewali—corresponding to the Durga Puja in Bengal—or the Hindoo Festival of Lights, with the worship and adulation of

Mammon for its aim and end, and dedicated to Lukshimi (the Goddess of wealth.)

Groups of drunken, highly excited Nepalese formed here and there about us, and among the neighboring houses, shouting at the top of their voices, and gambling, a pastime we were told not allowed even in Nepal territory, except during the festival of Dewali.

At times it seemed as though we had fallen into a crowd of madmen, whose uproar was greatly aggravated by the unusual excitement of the village dogs as they barked and howled at their drunken masters.

Long before dawn the next morning we were only too glad to get away. We plunged at once into the heavy jungle, which at that dark, early hour presented a very uninviting appearance, with the branches wet and dripping in consequence of the heavy mist, and the invisible depths harboring, as is well known, every denizen of the forest from the ponderous elephant and treacherous tiger to the poisonous snake and venomous scorpion.

By sun-rise we had made five miles and passed the Adhabhar, or half-way house, a

ADHABHAR, OR HALF-HOUSE IN THE DANGEROUS TERAI.

solitary wooden and masonry structure built to shelter travellers.

Alongside were one or two thatched huts with a ruined stone tank close by. The road for most of the way lay along the rough, rocky, dry bed of a monsoon stream, and was so straight in some places that one could look ahead for a mile or more, the tall trees on either side making a perfect avenue, as though cut out and trimmed to form the entrance into an immense park, while in the distant perspective their branches and trunks apparently came together and closed up the road.

These trees, straight as an arrow and shooting up 60 to 100 feet, are largely "sal" (*Shorea robusta*), a most enduring, substantial wood, superior to the famous Burmah teak for most building purposes. By reason of their great value they form the source of a very large income to the Nepal Government.

CHAPTER VI.

WE ENTER THE HIMALAYAS.

By 9 o'clock we came to an abrupt termination of the immense forest belt of the Terai, and to an equally sudden termination of the dead level of the plain; for the hills and their rising spurs began to show above the forest tops just as we had ascended the first little rise in the ground.

Immediately in front of us was the small village of Bechakho with a very large, well-built Powah on a high bank overlooking the wide pebbly bed of what must be in the rainy season a considerable river, but which at that time contained only a narrow stream of water as clear as crystal.

The whole aspect of the country was now changed as if by magic. Mountains towered before us, steep conical hills clothed in pines (*Pinus Kasya*) were all about us. The wretched cart track, too, had come to an end, and our cartman and the owner of the two ponies were dismissed with buksheesh. We now looked about for coolies. The few insignificant huts that composed the village did not give much promise of help.

It is at such times that we have wondered what the boastful Anglo-Indian official would do to extricate himself, propped up as he now is by every conceivable help, and backed by the strong arm of a powerful Government, which goes before him a protecting cloud by day and a providing pillar of fire by night. Whole towns and States are made to dance attendance upon him and his minutest wants are anticipated. What wonder then that he can travel, and yet he often makes most wretched work of it. It is stated that the British boundary commission which had been arranging the lines of demarcation with the Russians to limit their further encroachment upon Afghanistan and to prevent their nearer approach to India was supplied with such an extravagant amount of provisions, including champagne and other wines, together with such a lavish camp outfit and attendants as in any other nation would have been sufficient in outlay to maintain a good-sized army on the war path during the same period of time. Some estimate may be made of the "get-up" of this Commission when it is known that its chief, Sir Peter Lumsden, drew a monthly allowance of 41,000 rupees, (about £3,000 or $15,000!) The army impedimenta—a result of the excessive outlay of this expedition—caused great delay and difficulty in transport.

But to return to Bechakho—we resigned oursevles as composedly as possible to our situation, and succeeded in getting some milk, eggs and fowls from the village. After finishing a late breakfast, we strolled about and got into conversation with a buffalo herdsman, the owner of a large drove of milch buffaloes, who seemed to be in very good circumstances.

We asked him what he did with so much milk in the jungle, so far away from any large market. He replied that his people boiled the milk and made ghee or native butter, which they accumulated until there was enough to make it worth their while for one or more of his men to trudge a long distance to the most promising market. He complained, however, that there was great anxiety, exposure and risk in his business from the number of wild beasts prowling about, and he informed us that only a few days previous a tiger had killed a fine buffalo calf in one direction and a valuable buffalo cow in another, all within a mile of the place where we were. He wished we would go after these tigers, he would go along and help us; at the same time he remarked that there was no use in trying to hunt such sneaks without elephants, the grass in the jungles being eight and ten feet high, rendering all shooting impossible if not absolutely dangerous.

After wandering about for some time, we came upon an active, officious looking little fellow, who said he belonged to the set of post carriers, or "dak runners" as they are called, who are stationed every six miles all the way to Khatmandu for the purpose of carrying the daily mail-bag from Segowli, on the arrival there of the train. These runners do the distance of 96 miles in fair weather in a little over twenty-six hours, each runner going at a dog trot over his beat of six miles and then delivering the letter bag together with a little tin box (which we afterwards learned contained the Resident's bread) to the next runner. This lithe, active individual, with the hope of reward, at once interested himself in our behalf, and to our great surprise, within an hour or two, had a motley collection of men, women and children gathered in front of us, among whom our bags, bedding and bundles were properly distributed, when we again took up the line of march as though nothing had happened and plunged into a most picturesque wild gorge full of chattering monkeys and green pigeons.

Our swarthy little champion, not liking the idea of our walking, had procured two miserable apologies of ponies, which we were persuaded to try to ride, but we found walking easier and dismissed the scarecrows; and salaming our estimable helper in a way he appreciated as fully as we had esteemed his

COOLIE GIRLS AND THEIR BASKETS.

services, we hastened on after our motley caravan. The walking was most tedious and difficult as we picked our way past boulders, over rocks and through yielding, rough sand; and unless we constantly noted every footstep, which obliged us to give up gazing on the beauty of the scenery on every hand, we were sure to stub our toes or take a header into some uncompromising fact in front of us.

For the first few miles we had to thread our way up along the dry portion of the bed of the stream already referred to as passing by Bechakho, whose water made such a noise rushing over the stones and reverberating among the towering cliffs, that it drowned all sounds in its deafening uproar and made talking too laborious, if not quite impossible.

As evening began to approach, the sun tints on the mountain tops and the deepening shadows below completely exhausted all powers of admiration.

We passed a large caravan of bullocks laden, some with betel nuts, others with sheets of copper, and others still with bales of cloth, their owners having stopped to prepare their encampment for the night beside a group of pine trees, as they dared not proceed further for fear of darkness setting in. They advised us also to halt but we wished to make all the progress possible and so pushed on; in fact while talking with the bullock drivers our servant and some of the coolies had already passed us, so we hastened our steps hoping to overtake them.

Of course we met no one, nor were there any settlements along our route, so we marched on in silence until darkness settled down upon us in earnest. Walking now took more the form of groping, and the repeated stumblings, bumps and raps we got made our gradual progress upwards very slow and difficult.

Just as we began to wonder what had become of our servant and the coolies who had preceded us, we espied a light ahead, and on coming up to it through the gloom, found it to be a fire built by our servant, who, with the coolies had become quite alarmed in the darkness and dared not go any further; so they stopped on the path where they had become benighted, made a fire and huddled about it, determined to pass the night just where they were. There was no use in complaining that we could not put up in such an unlikely feverish spot without the least shelter, with the night wind howling through the gorge as if moaning for the lost, playing a requiem of its own on the overhanging pines, set to the tune that is sung by the surges of a distant ocean on a storm beaten coast. The foaming torrent too, whose rocky bed we were ascending, chimed in with notes in keeping with its hoarse voice, so that picture our situation as best one might, it was decidedly an awkward one. We expostulated with our servant but he declared with feelings akin to fear that there was no alternative, as the nearest place with any shelter was the village of Hetowda ten miles distant, and that it was quite impossible to reach that in the darkness.

While he said this, crouched up beside the fire, he turned and took a nervous look at the surrounding forest, muttered something about his "Kismet" or fate that had brought him into such a fix, and warned us in an undertone not even to suggest making a further move, assuring us that this would at once occasion a general stampede back, among our dozen coolies, whose staring eyes and ivory teeth were the only distinguishable objects about as they glistened in the reflected fire-light, forming a weird contrast to their swarthy ill clad bodies a subject worthy of the pencil of a Doré.

Seeing there was no way but to submit to our enforced situation, we ordered our bags to be unstrapped, our beds to be unfolded, built one or two more fires, got our water to boil, drank our tea without milk and ate our supper with thankfulness, and in the spirit of contentment laid ourselves down on our cots (our coolies were already snoring away, sprawled out upon the ground) being far too tired to be bothered with any unpleasant reflections suggested by our exposed situation.

We soon passed into the land of rest and fairy dreams, the last sensation of consciousness that I can recall being the sound of Harry's voice (I had supposed him to be already asleep) saying with a yawn, as he wrapped his warm covering closer about him, "Do you ever think when putting up at any of our fine New York or London hotels, with gas and electric lights turned on, of such first-class accommodation as this?"

CHAPTER VII.

A STARTLING EXPERIENCE.

We were up the next morning by dawn that revealed our "first-class accommodation" to be of the wildest description conceivable. What most concerned us, however, was to find ourselves none the worse for the night's bivouac.

We started but had hardly gone fifty yards when a most extraordinary spectacle greeted our eyes as well as our sense of smell. There lay before us, blocking up the pathway, the carcass of an immense elephant, his legs sticking up in the air like the tall stumps on freshly cleared land, while his body and trunk lay stiffened and mortifying, the only mourner being a large carrion vulture (Gyps Bengalensis) so well known in India for spying a dainty funeral miles and miles away. There he sat on a tall commanding pine, the personification of hypochondria, evidently ruminating on the uncertainty of life, and how the mighty had fallen.

We did not disturb him in his meditations but left him to the diversion of his gloomy thoughts.

The elephant had evidently been dead only a few hours, for his skin was quite intact, but decomposition had already made progress, as was evident from the sound of the seething gases escaping from his huge body just as if the carcass were being roasted over a fire, and also from the offensive odor, which luckily for us had been wafted by the wind away from our encampment during the night; otherwise we should have been driven from the spot, bag and baggage, most unceremoniously by a foe of which none of us, with the most lively imagination, had the faintest conception. I am positive had a live elephant come crushing down upon us through the forest, not one of us would have thought it at all strange; indeed the coolies with bated breath had spoken of such an occurrence as not unlikely, but to encounter and be overpowered by a dead elephant was the height of absurdity.

We laughed, held our noses, and with great difficulty made a detour over the rocks and boulders around the carcass and proceeded on our march.

A little more than a mile brought us to Chirriaghata, a low sandstone range over which the path is carried by a deep, narrow fissure in the sandy soil, thereby reducing the climb. At the top, in an excavation made in the side of the fissure, we came upon a Hindoo deity with a brazen face and front, beside which was the ever-present Mahadeo's phallic linga (the Hindoo's Creator) all bedecked with tinsel and flowers, and strewn with rice and copper coins, the votive offerings of the sin-laden as they filter through this first Nepalese pass.

This mountain shrine was attended by a bright Newar boy not over fourteen, who told us in reply to our many inquiries, that he had been there all alone two years; that his home was miles away beyond certain lofty ranges, but that a family in a hut just at the foot of the pass we had ascended took care of him, and that he had nothing to fear as he was engaged in the meritorious duty of custodian to the Gods, an instance of faith that would cause a good many examples of modern Christianity to suffer by comparison.

The ascending path by which we had come now. descended as abruptly on the other side into the dry rocky channel of a mountain torrent that wended its way in the opposite direction from the one we had just come. After a mile of very rough walking, we came upon what appeared to be a faint attempt at a good, wide-made road free from stones, leading at a gently inclined gradient, through a beautiful forest of very uniformly developed young, slender, tapering sal trees.

After some three miles of this rather pleasant walk we came to the full flowing, yet narrow stream of Kurru, crossed by an old, but well-made, sal log bridge.

We began now to pass numbers of coolies, attended by sepoy guards of the British Government, carrying all sorts of camp articles, such as tents, folding tables, chairs, carpets and everything requisite to make one comfortable. There must have been a little army of coolies, a number of whom having been pressed into service against their will, took every opportunity to get behind a bush or tree, dodge the guards, drop their burdens and bolt into the jungles.

In various secluded spots we came upon a deserted bed and chair here, an abandoned washstand or basin there, and so on; strange things to find in the wilds of the jungle. All this turn out, we presently learned, belonged to the British Resident, or English consular officer deputed by his Government to watch British interests at the Court of Nepal.

This officer was on his way to Segowli to attend to certain boundary questions; we were told that we should meet him at our next halting ground, which place was the village of Hetowda, about two miles beyond Kurru log bridge, where we arrived by nine o'clock that morning, and found the largest and best kept Powah of any on the road.

Then, too, the village was a very good sized one for the jungle, but like a number of other inhabited places along our route, it was only a winter settlement, for from the first of May

HETOWDA POWAH OR CARAVANSERY,
FAMOUS RENDEZVOUS FOR TIGER SHOOTING.

to the end of October the place is abandoned to the deadly orgies of the Terai fever, to the loathsome leech and the filthy rhinoceros. Even the Nepalese Custom House located here, and which during the winter months collects quite an amount of duty on merchandise passing through, closes its doors in summer and retires further into the interior.

Here too nearly all the caravans of bullocks, ponies and donkeys coming from India turn and go back, leaving their burdens to be carried further on by coolies, owing to the difficulties of the road.

The Powah of Hetowda, we found to be a commodious, well-constructed two-storied building in the form of a square surrounding an open court, the prevailing caravansery style so common in the East. We found quite a number of such buildings at various intervals all along our route, and whether built by the Nepalese Government or by private enterprise, their construction is deemed most meritorious. They certainly are a great boon to travellers.

In front of the Hetowda Powah were numbers of people, coolies, servants, sepoys, *et hoc omne genus*, all busily engaged in making preparations for the early anticipated arrival of the Resident.

The thought occurred to us then, as it had on many previous occasions, that travelling must be made easy to officials with so many to prepare the way and get all things ready beforehand.

Our own servant, coolies and effects had not yet come up, and while hesitating about trying to get shelter at some place other than the Powah, for fear of taking up room to which the Resident we felt should have first claim, certain of the servants came up and politely conducted us to a pleasant upstairs room, saying there was abundant accommodation, and their sahib would by no means require all.

Our coolies now arrived bringing our things, and we were soon comfortably settled.

By noon the Resident came, borne by coolies, seated in a jampan, or sort of sedan chair with a straight handle before and behind, that rested on their shoulders.

Later in the day I called on him and found him very pleasant and affable. He thought it rather bold and venturesome in us to undertake in a private capacity such a difficult trip, declaring that he found it hard enough, although an officer and commanding every possible help; at the same time he confessed that we seemed to get over the ground much more easily than he did, for he had no end of trouble with his coolies, who kept running away and throwing down their loads at every turn in the road, causing him great inconvenience and delay. He inquired whether any one had tried to stop us since entering Nepal territory, and when we told him no, he mentioned a place, Cisagurdi, about eighteen miles ahead, where a strong guard of Nepalese soldiers, stationed in a steep pass, questioned every one going by, and were disposed to stop any foreigner, especially Europeans not having strong official permits from Khatmandu. He did not think, however, that we would be interfered with as I was already provided with his official perwana or passport, and to make it sure he promised to send orders by a returning messenger that we must not be stopped, or our progress questioned. Just before parting the Resident laughingly remarked that one of the greatest desires of his life was to see America. I expressed the hope that he would do so, as he would see something on a great scale. "Yes," he laughingly continued, "but then I should not feel easy, for you know everybody carries a revolver over there and doesn't hesitate to use it!"

THE LATE SIR JUNG BAHADUR AND WIFE.

CHAPTER VIII.

A BEAUTIFUL ROAD: CHANGING COOLIES.

Early the next morning having dismissed our coolies and taken a fresh set (the Resident taking the opposite direction) we were off. Our march that day was the pleasantest of the whole journey, being along the bank of the foaming Rapti, and over a level well-made road, in many places cut out of the solid rock, the work of the great Sir Jung Bahadur, Nepal's late prime minister; and but for some bad breaks here and there made by the monsoon, it was good enough for a four-in-hand to be driven at full speed for a distance of over ten miles.

The first two miles brought us to a large tributary of the Rapti, over which was a long log bridge resting on eight or ten log piers, built like log cabins and filled with sand and stone. This bridge was now unfortunately useless, having had one of the centre piers carried away during the last rains, making a great gap in the roadway, so that a diversion had to be constructed through the rough bed of the river, which it is to be hoped is only temporary pending the early repair of such a good bridge.

Six miles beyond, after passing through a fine bit of Himalayan scenery, we came to another and smaller bridge and to the village of Bheisardwar, in a very narrow part of the valley, with mountains running up into the clouds on both sides and covered with rank forests. Here our coolies put down their loads saying they would go no further, but easily finding another set, we paid them off and let them go.

In another two miles we reached the large Powah of Nowarta with its few huts scattered about making up the village. Here we grudgingly made a long wearisome halt, as our new batch of men declared they had come their regular beat, and having done all that could be legally required of them, they laid down their burdens and quietly departed without even stopping for their money Such leave taking was rather abrupt, but was explained by the fact of its being the last and great day of Dewali, when, as at our Christmas, everybody was supposed to be merrymaking. At any rate everyone we met seemed to be either drunk, or intoxicated with the excitement of gambling, and was rigidly averse to work of any kind, a spirit which had affected our coolies as well.

Then too the rule which holds throughout the East that each town *must* furnish coolies to the traveller (he can claim as many as he brings) to the next town only and no further, should they object to going, obliged us to submit to the desertion of our men. We tried to get others, but the place seemed to be deserted.

After a couple of hours search we found two men, two women and a boy, who agreed to carry what they could to Bhimphedi, a town five miles ahead. They could, however, only carry about half of our effects, and though not knowing when we could procure more help, we started them off unattended. And be it said touching the proverbial honesty of these poor creatures, that we had not the slighest fear of our luggage being tampered with although they carried money and valuables that were accessible in bags and bundles.

We now renewed our efforts to get the rest of our things off, and in looking about we spied a group of men behind some bushes, gathered about a buffalo they had just butchered beside the Rapti, which they were cutting up for a feast that night. Going up we found the head man of the village there, and told him that he was bound to help us. He promised to do so, went off with the party about him and that was the last we saw of him.

Finding ourselves thus nicely trapped, with half our goods already gone on, and the other half lying by the roadside, also noticing the shadows creeping up the valley along which our road lay, caused by the sun having already set behind a neighboring peak and rapidly sinking, we were warned of approaching night.

There was now no alternative but to leave our servant in charge, enjoining upon him to come as quickly as he could get the coolies, while we ourselves hastened on to Bhimphedi. Disturbed as we were at the thought of our forlorn situation, both of us started up in a fit of desperation and, as we walked off, snatched up a few light articles to carry ourselves, such as a box of tinned biscuits, a lantern, a rifle, or a courier bag, and began to plod along.

We soon gave up talking as the roar of the Rapti on our right grew louder and drowned our voices, so we proceeded in silence. Darkness too came on apace, while the night wind began to feel chilly, showing that we were rising into a higher and cooler atmosphere.

At this juncture I happened to cast my eyes beyond the noisy stream to where the forest coming down from an immense height touched the water's edge and saw through the gloom a dark object moving along slowly among the boulders and drifted logs. Being a hundred yards off, I could not readily distinguish, for want of more light, the nature of the object, when suddenly we noticed it mount a rock and give a furious plunge into the midst of the foaming torrent.

We stopped, expecting to see it borne down by the rapidity of the current and dashed to pieces among the eddying whirlpools. Nothing of the kind! To our amazement up rose the black thing—a large bear—from under, the seething waters, then reached out both its fore paws and by an astonishing exhibition of strength clutched the bank a few feet below us.

The situation was not without its dangers, because the Himalayan bear (*ursus labiatus*) has a sinister reputation of its own, which it must be confessed it tries very hard to justify. Still, although it was rather close quarters the Winchester which my son held made the contest more even, and as I stretched out my hand for the rifle I watched the brute approach still nearer with some degree of equanimity. I had met many other members of the same family face to face before and could depend on my nerves and my aim.

I had not taken my eyes off the bear and was still holding out my hand for the rifle when my son called out, in a horror-stricken voice, "we have left the cartridges behind."

Here was a situation! My cheeks burned, even as I faced the bear, at the unsportsmanlike oversight.

But there was no time for reflection, for Bruin was already on his hind legs and seeking closer quarters. What should I do? Club him with the rifle? a poor game to play with a bear and abandoned as soon as thought of.

As I glanced hastily around for a weapon I caught sight of a large water-worn stone which appeared to promise some merits as a missile if I could only bring it to bear upon that thick skull in front of me.

For a moment the bear stopped in his advance as if it suddenly occurred to him as strange that we did not run away while we had the chance and that there might be some kind of trap for him somewhere. His hesitation, which did not last more than a couple of seconds, was sufficient for me to poise and launch, with desperate effort, the heavy stone which by great good fortune struck him full on the head just above the small vicious eyes which seemed to spring together in a horrid squint as the huge stone struck him.

A piercing howl of pain, which rose high above the roar of the torrent, followed the blow, and for an instant the bear reeled half unconscious, clutched the air desperately with his paws and then fell on all fours.

But the stupifying effect was only momentary. Like a flash he rose on his hind legs again and with a fury in his little vicious eyes which boded no good for me if he could only get hold of me. Still it would appear that the terrible blow had to some extent demoralized him as well as shaken his courage. Possibly he reflected that there were more of the same kind in store for him. Anyhow there we were still in front of him and not running away as everything else did which he met excepting his good friends the Elephant and Rhinoceros.

While one might count three he stood in a picturesque position of hesitating menace, fronting me with fury in his eyes, and then he suddenly turned and with a tremendous leap plunged once more into the foaming waters and was lost to sight.

There was no doubt that we had had great

luck with our bear for the situation was one of considerable danger, unarmed as we were. Fortunately, we did not know our defenseless condition until we were, so to speak, in the thick of the fight and then action banished all thought of fear.

There was nothing further to do but to walk along in a sadder and wiser frame of mind, taking a solemn vow never to leave cartridges behind and if we did, then invariably to leave the gun too—a lesson we had already supposed ourselves to have learned long, long ago, and yet the simple neglect of which under the present circumstances had cost us the loss of a beautiful bear's skin.

CHAPTER IX.

DELAYED AT BHIMPHEDI.

Darkness intensified by the surrounding forests now overwhelmed us, and but for the cheerful rays of a little lantern we had taken the precaution to bring we should have had to get down under some trees and there sit the night out.

On and on we walked along a road with many turnings but seemingly with no ending. Twice we crossed streams by means of stepping-stones, and at length coming suddenly on some huts we earnestly hoped we had reached Bhimphedi, our intended camping place, to which the coolies who had preceded us were instructed to go. In this we were disappointed, being told that we had still two miles further to travel.

So on we went, and presently passed through a thick clump of trees loaded with a species of wild fruit that was being resorted to by some large animals, presumably bears and pigs, for they scampered off in the darkness making a great noise, evidently not liking our lantern.

The two miles still left for us to march, seemed to lengthen into double that distance before, weary and hungry, we reached the village of Bhimphedi at 9 p.m. Here we found our coolies and the things they had brought safely located in the small open veranda of the house of the Naik or chief police officer of the town, and here we concluded to pass the night, being too tired to seek other quarters.

On examining the coolies' loads, we found that our bedding had been left behind with our servant and the rest of our belongings, though a basket of provisions and some dishes had come on; by the help of which, together with good milk obtained for us in the village, we made out a comfortable supper.

It was now nearly midnight, and yet no signs of our servant or the articles left in his charge. So throwing ourselves right on the floor of the veranda, with our saddles for pillows, we tried to secure some sleep.

For two reasons we did not rest well; one was insufficient covering against the chilliness of the night air, and the other was a constant stream of singing beggars, the night being the last of Dewali (corresponding to our New Year's eve), when everybody seemed privileged to go to anybody's quarters and rouse him from his slumbers by giving him a New Year's serenade, during which every line of their lugubrious song was made to end with the refrain "Dou-cee-rae," "Dou-cee-rae," and interspersed with loud importunate demands for gifts.

This kind of performance each strolling party repeated and kept up till something was granted them in the shape of either grain, food, clothing or coppers. As this went on the whole night through, we were only too glad to bestir ourselves by early dawn and start up our circulation by walking briskly to and fro.

We now anxiously waited for our servant and luggage. Up to noon nothing came, so procuring a pony in the town for Harry, he mounted and rode back to look up the servant.

Meanwhile I availed myself of the opportunity to jot down some notes of our journey. The veranda we occupied commanded an interesting view of the village, the valley of the Rapti we had been ascending and a circular range of perpendicular cliffs of great height that abruptly ended this valley.

Just below the veranda was a spring whose water ran out of a stone spout fashioned like a griffin, and fell in a continuous stream a few feet below on a linga, or one of the emblematic forms of Mahadeo (Siva).

These animal-shaped water spouts are called Dhara. Their construction, like the building of Powahs, is regarded as an especially meritorious act, entitling the founder to the richest blessings of heaven.

Beside the griffin spout exposed to every change of weather sat a man, a "sadhu," almost nude, in the prime of life, and, though blind, endeavoring to follow the course of the sun from sunrise to sunset with his sightless eyeballs while mumbling over his beads of the rough *rudraksha* or deep marked seeds of the *Eleocarpus ganitrus.* At night he would partake of the alms bestowed on him during the day by passers-by and lie down on a rough piece of gunny cloth or burlap just where he had been sitting, and fall asleep only to wake the next morning to repeat the same monotonous devotions. Such had been his occupation for the past five years, and such would it continue to be till released by death.

Three hours had gone by and no sign of either Harry or the servant, so I thought of going to look them up myself, when I spied a curious looking object coming along the road, which soon proved to be our bundle of bedding on the back of our servant, who had turned himself into a coolie, the most creditable act I ever saw him do, thereby covering a multitude of subsequent failures, any one of which might have merited his instant dismissal. He had a gloomy story to relate of how he sat up all the cold night through, watching beside our things left on the road; how he had been frightened by wild beasts, how in the morning when renewing his efforts

NEPALESE MOTHER CARRYING HER BABE.

no coolies could be got for love or money, and how in sheer desperation picking up our bedding and getting an old man to watch in his place, he had come on like a common coolie himself. He passed my son about half-way, who told him to hasten on and he would fetch the remainder of what was left in some way.

Another two hours passed, and then another weary one, seemingly as long as the first two. Still no one appeared coming over the silent road, and as it now began growing dark, I set out myself to walk back. I had hardly gone a mile, when whom should I come upon but my son Harry walking beside his pony, the latter carrying all that he could get strapped on him. There were still three coolies' loads remaining behind, but Harry had managed to find a man who had agreed for buksheesh to have all our things brought on that night, which he did two hours later.

We had now lost a day, but we planned that the following marches should make up for it. That night we passed more comfortably than the previous one and were up before dawn, being waked by our coolies, whom I had already made sure of in the village, and who insisted on a very early start, as the march was to be a very hard one, right up over a pass 6,447 feet above sea level and over 4,000 feet above our location.

CHAPTER X.

CLIMBING CISAGURDI.

Our path up the Pass of Bhimphedi was a narrow zigzag and very stony, so that the ascent was laborious and slow, and, what aggravated matters was Harry's early developing a burning fever, the immediate result of his efforts yesterday, and a remote cause being malaria which he had contracted at our exposed camp near the dead elephant. He, however, bravely trudged on, though stopping with increasing frequency to catch breath and to rest. This gave us opportunity to admire at every ascending step the widening prospect, and feel the air rapidly growing cooler and more bracing.

At a commanding point after an ascent of some 3,000 feet we looked down, and there almost in a line with our feet. nestled the village of Bhimphedi, consisting of a single street, lined on both sides by low tiled houses, the whole divided from the plain beyond by a wide stretch of sand and stone, the dry bed of the Rapti, said to contain a large stream of water which flowed a few feet under the surface and broke out a mile or so below, forming the boisterous torrent along which we had been marching.

Bhimphedi marked an abrupt termination of the Rapti valley, as was apparent from the precipitous ranges we were climbing, and which formed above the village a complete *cul-de-sac* in which suddenly ended the level road already referred to, made by Nepalese soldiers acting under orders from Sir Jung Bahadur twenty years ago.

What the original intentions were of bringing a splendid level road up to the foot of an almost insurmountable pass, which could not be cleared save by climbing, is a mystery.

Another steady pull up of about 1,000 feet (the coolies whistling a hoarse monotonous note every few steps from habit, when taking breath), brought us to a low, and somewhat dilapidated, stone wall, with bastions and a

BHIMPHEDI VILLAGE AND SUBTERRANEAN RIVER AT FOOT OF SISSAGURRI PASS.

gateway, (but no gate,) apparently hanging on for dear life to the faintest effort at a spur which nature in some wild freak had thrust out from the precipitous overhanging mountain sides.

As we entered this forlorn enclosure by winding around through loopholed walls and débris, we took in the situation at once. To our left were a few huts which clung to this wild, contracted perch. These were chiefly the dwellings of the garrison stationed here by the Nepal Government to guard this difficult pass, and were clustered about a tile-roofed bungalow, built for the accommodation of Nepalese chiefs and well-to-do travellers in their journeyings to and from Khatmandu. Here the British Resident himself had stopped the night before we met him at Hetowda, as already narrated.

To our immediate right, and fringing the pathway by which we had entered, was an apparently bottomless valley, which made one's head turn in attempting to fathom it by craning the neck over its perpendicular walls of rock. Just ahead of us, and barring the exit from this garrisoned enclosure, against any further progress up the mountain, were five light poles running horizontally across into slotted posts on each side, exactly like pasture bars at home and rather poor ones at that.

Here beside these bars paced a Gurkha sentry, the first military sign we had been treated to in military Nepal. He was armed with a loaded musket and clothed in a faded red English uniform, and his appearance created an impression that here our advance would be questioned before those bars would be let down for us to pass.

I need hardly add that a better site could not have been chosen for guarding this highway from India into Nepal. Imagine a precipitous chain of mountains, a slight projection of a spur thrust out from the mountain side and forming a shelf just large enough to hold a small cluster of huts, a zigzag path running almost perpendicular in parts up the mountain, between dangerous precipices; imagine such a formidable spot and no alternative but to pass over this spur guarded by a handful of dare-devils of Gurkhas, who could stop a whole invading army from advance, as even British troops can testify, and the reader will have some idea of our surroundings and the peculiar situation which confronted us on that bright crisp morning under a brilliant sun and overtopping snow-capped peaks. Such was our introduction to this forbidden land and to this travel forbidding people.

Our arrival had caused a stir in the guard-house. Our coolies had been stopped by the sentry on duty and sat down to catch breath, with their burdens beside them. Harry lay groaning on the ground, resting his head on a stone, flushed deeply by the intensity of his fever, and with a pulse above a hundred.

Just then the Havildar, or chief officer, in charge of the garrison, came out in undress uniform, and without the customary salam, accosted us abruptly. This was a breach of the commonest oriental courtesy, and did not augur well. He rudely asked where we were going. I replied, to Khatmandu. He wanted to know on whose authority. I told him I had a perwana or passport. He asked me to produce it, saying he had had no intimation of our coming. This I knew to be false, for word had been sent by the Resident, to my knowledge, from Hetowda, through returning messengers, and I myself had forewarned the Havildar of our approach from Bhimphedi, at the bottom of the pass, while detained there for two days as already stated.

I had no sooner handed the perwana to this officious chief than he tossed it aside, saying it was no good. I was somewhat annoyed and replied that he could not read (which was a fact) and requested that his Brahmin scribe or writer be summoned. He said it made no difference; he did not recognize British authority; that the perwana was not worth the paper it was written on, as he saw no seal of his government on it.

I firmly insisted on the Brahmin's being called, and while one of the many sepoys that had now gathered around us went for the scribe, I took up the perwana and began to read myself aloud the Devnagiri character in which the passport was written.

This somewhat astonished the Havildar and he muttered something about my being a strange sahib who talked and read the vernacular in common with the natives.

As the Brahmin with his reed pen (the veritable calamus of the ancient Romans) and country-made paper and ink approached, I ordered him to make a copy of the perwana, somewhat to the surprise of his chief, that I should take it upon myself to give orders, thereby assuming the function of the superior officer in command.

This, however, was nothing compared to what immediately followed. While the Brahmin was copying the perwana seated on the ground, with the thigh and knee of his right leg raised to support the paper, I gazed at the motley garrison, numbering at least fifty sepoys, all of whom were crowding around us, some in old and faded uniforms like the sentry at the bars, others hardly awake and with only a cloth thrown about their dusky forms. In their excitement they brandished their arms and, headed by their gruff chief, they formed a weird and menacing group in this strange eyrie.

In front stood or rather squatted the timid coolies with our still more timid servant, while Harry lay beside my feet on the ground, mumbling as though his brain was being affected. Knowing the rapid and possibly fatal consequences of the fever, this last sight decided matters for me. Seeing, moreover, no disposition to yield on the part of the natives who had intercepted our progress and wishing to save time while the perwana was being copied, I suddenly arose from the rock which had formed my seat, made my way silently but with a determination that quickly cleared a path for me, took the bars down one by one and in a commanding tone ordered my servant and the coolies to proceed at once up the pass.

The coolies hesitated a moment, not knowing whether to fear me or the garrison most. But a look at my desperate face seemed to help them to decide, and taking up their loads they started off quietly in Indian file, headed by my servant.

A momentary silence fell upon the garrison as I returned and resumed my seat beside the

Brahmin and the Havildar chief. The latter looked the picture of astonishment, but his look soon changed to one of contemptuous derision as he recalled his own power and our helplessness.

A better, fiercer specimen of the Gurkha type as personified in this chief could not have been found, and no doubt he was stationed at this important point on account of his marked personal characteristics. A short, thick-set man of the average height of his race (5 feet 4 inches), about fifty years of age; broad-shouldered, deep-chested, with sinews of iron, resembling the stunted weather-beaten oaks of his Himalayan home; his face pitted deeply with small-pox and further disfigured by an old savage gash down his cheek-bone, long since healed though badly put together —such was the Havildar, a thorough specimen of a human tiger, whom I now felt I must beard in his very den.

By way of explanation I ought to say that the Havildar and his garrison, in keeping with their encouraged aversion to foreigners visiting their country, were bent on making the most of a political technicality to prevent our further advance, even though it should be temporary only. This technicality was the neglect to have our passport viséd by the Nepal Government, the propriety of which I did not for one moment question.

I had already pointed out to the Resident at Hetowda this omission by his Department, but he had assured me that all would be right. Besides, the garrison knew full well, as I had explained to them that it would be monstrous to suppose that the Resident would permit what the Nepal Durbar or court would not sanction; that I had done my utmost to prevent just such a predicament as we were now in, and had taken every possible precaution to shield the garrison from any blame on our account. And, now, because somebody had been remiss in duty at the British Residency before forwarding us our passport, it was very unjust that we should be made to suffer in this way.

My object in writing at such length of this matter is owing to what I was aware involved a grave political principle, and on account of certain opinions expressed afterwards, when the matter was brought to the notice of the British authorities; and though happily I was able to explain away all disagreeableness to the entire satisfaction of the Nepal Court, there still lingered a disposition among the former to blame me for acting injudiciously, if not high-handedly.

Only a few, and those few who have had bitter experience themselves, will fully comprehend my uncomfortable position, aggravated as it was by the results of a systematic and determined opposition on the part of the British Government in India (contrary to its general principles) against all European travel and commercial intercourse on the frontier of its Indian Empire. A short-sighted, brainless policy that has fostered in that dark corner of the earth ignorance and exclusiveness, and nourished bigotry, conceit, suspicion, hatred of the Feringhi, and the most mischievous of false notions, that has already cost England no end of trouble and expense, and is bound to brew for her still greater troubles and expense in the future.

The Russians manage affairs better from their side.* One intelligent European traveller, one conciliating Vilayati (white) merchant, one faithful pioneer missionary in a centre of darkness, has disbanded a regiment of fanatics and dispelled a whole army of misconceptions.†

* The following extract from a leading Bombay paper indicates the very different methods adopted by Russia under similar circumstances, and in relation to this neutral belt: "A St. Petersburg correspondent writes 'The great market at Nishni-Novgorod which has just been closed has this year brought several new and interesting facts to light, illustrating in a remarkable manner the beneficial results which Russia has obtained from her Central Asian conquests. Large territories, which only a few years ago were inhabited but by wild robbers, are being transformed into peaceful trading countries. The new Transcaspian Railway promises wonders in this way. Thanks to this railway, Persia, Khiva, Bokhara, and Turkestan were largely represented at the Nishni-Novgorod market this year as never before. Thanks to this same railway large quantities of Russian goods of every kind on the road to the different countries of Central Asia were in the market. The freights are not very heavy.'"

† THOMAS STEVENS, the special correspondent of *Outing*, while making a tour of the world on a bicycle, was checked while penetrating Afghanistan, and wrote to a personal friend:

"You have heard, perhaps, that while I was a prisoner at Herat I wrote Col. Ridgeway, of the Boundary Commission, asking him, if possible, to assist me through to India, and that for answer the Governor of Herat received instructions to escort me back into Persia. I have met English travellers and others since, who think Col. R. might have assisted me through that intervening few hundred miles, knowing that I had ridden from San Francisco to get there. Col. R. doubtless knows the reason for ignoring my request better than anybody else does, and the difficulties of the situation are probably greater than most people imagine. I saw quite enough in Afghanistan to understand why nobody, and particularly no newspaper correspondents are allowed in there at the present time, and could write an article on what I saw that would no doubt create something of a sensation in London; but, of course, I should be sorry to allow anything to escape me

CHAPTER XI.

ENCOUNTER WITH THE HAVILDAR.

Our Perwana had by this time been copied, and the copy well sprinkled with sand—the usual blotter of the natives.

I took my document and arose. The Havildar looked at me and demanded what I was going to do. I pointed to my sick boy and then to the coolies ahead, a good way up near the summit of the pass, and said in the most polite of Oriental diction that time was pressing, the difficulties of the journey were great, and that I must hasten on.

"No," said the Havildar, "you cannot pro-

---

that might perhaps tend to aggravate the situation of affairs on the frontier. I cannot help thinking, however, that had it happened to be anybody less favorable to our interests in Afghanistan than myself that had penetrated thus far behind the scenes, it might have been as well to have treated him with a little more courtesy than to have him unceremoniously bounced out of the country. These thoughts occurred to me the other day in Tiflis, when a Russian officer, of sufficient influence and importance to be related to the Empress, approached me and tried to pump me concerning the roads and the nature of the country down below Herat."

ceed. You must stay here, I have already detained white men like you until they were either sent back, or until all technicalities for their further advance were overcome." I replied, "You cannot stop me." He smiled derisively, and ordered his men to form into line and see to their arms—more for effect than for anything else, I surmised.

Suiting my actions to the bustling of the men and the noise of their arms, I lifted Harry to his feet and deliberately pushed a passage through the crowd. Then, as I passed out beyond the bars, I turned and shouted out, "Salam to the Havildar Sahib!"

Nothing but my control of temper and my determination had stood me in good stead and helped us to clear ourselves. The garrison looked astounded, and the Havildar was the picture of blank amazement.

Something to the effect that here was the strangest Feringhi he had ever seen, passed his gritted teeth, followed by the mutterings of the garrison.

Even the coolies away up above us noticed our passing out through the bars in spite of the guards, and stopped to watch with evident anxiety the outcome of such action, while Harry himself realized that some ill-boding menace had been overcome, for he remarked: "It seems to me we had a pretty close shave through those bars!"

I made some response by way of enouragement, though I mentally confessed to a feeling of unpleasant misgivings lest we had not seen the last of our Havildar friend and his armed attendants.

Accordingly I urged the poor boy to quicken his pace, saying it would be advisable to put as much distance as possible between the garrison and ourselves.

The ascent was still steep, but not so bad as the portion we had already surmounted, and we hoped in another hour to reach the top of the pass. Half an hour dragged out its lagging minutes, as we plodded wearily on and up, and just as I was thinking how foolish I had been to indulge in any misgivings, we heard shoutings behind us, and turned to find the Havildar (this time in uniform and his sword belted about him) accompanied by half a dozen of his sentries, carrying their muskets, at times running and then walking, in their effort to overtake us.

At once I surmised their purport. They had evidently been thinking the matter over since we were allowed to pass, and had regretted their failure to offer us any serious resistance.

Up they came, panting, breathless, and rudely shouted, "You must go back with us." I turned and faced them sternly, and in a firm, but polite, tone required of them some reason for their unseemly pursuit of us. Then, addressing the Havildar, I asked if he took us for robbers, as any one would suppose we were, I said, judging from the threatening manner in which they had pursued us weapon in hand. Besides, had he not, only half an hour ago, tacitly acquiesced in our passing through his garrisoned enclosure? "No!" he shouted, "you must go back." I told him I would do nothing of the kind. "Well," he said, "I will make you, or take the consequences." At that he turned to his men and ordered them to approach with their weapons ready. This scene quite overcame Harry, and he tottered and sank to the ground. The coolies with our servant up in the pass stood stock still.

I now became fully aroused, and made no concealment of my outraged feelings. Turning upon my asailants, I looked angrily at the Havildar and hissed out, "You miserable wretch, it was not enough for you to come up alone and thus torment me, but you must bring a lot of fellow cowards with you, with drawn swords and loaded muskets!"

"I tell you that if that child of mine dies, by all your gods I will require his blood of each one of you; and as for you, the Havildar, the chiefest sinner of all, this time to-morrow I shall have audience with the Maharajah and require of him to send by hand of speedy messenger a platter, on which shall be carried back as atonement your bleeding head."

This last declaration struck my opponents as not only possible but quite probable, and had a wonderful effect on the Havildar. But the reader must not suppose I had over-awed this band of Gurkhas. "They are not built that way." Although they stand in dread of their rulers who possess the power of life and death and exercise it summarily they no more cared for me personally than the tiger for the victim he has seized.

The Gurkha, unlike his brother of India's plains—the mild, timid, rice-nurtured Hindoo—fights to the death against all odds, and deservedly scorns the appellation of coward.

I need hardly add that I was entirely unarmed as to my person beyond a light bamboo stick, as an alpenstock, and it was only while this dramatic scene was culminating that there flashed across my brain the recollection of a long-forgotten six-shooter—America's latest patent—packed away in my bag, and which might stand me in good stead should matters be pushed further. I must confess, however, that I had not the remotest idea of handling this weapon, being a thorough believer in persuasion over powder, so that such an extreme recourse was no sooner thought of than dismissed.

As stated, the Havildar was suddenly impressed with the probable realization of my threat, for without any special effort of the imagination he evidently saw his head passing along that same path on a platter on the top of another head—that of the coolie messenger—speeding back to his royal master. He at once changed his demeanor. He ordered his men to fall back, and in an altered tone and polite way asked if I would return to his garrison quarters.

"Ah, Havildar Sahib," I said, "you now talk like a respectable Gurkha—a brave people that I have always admired. Had you spoken to me in that way when first we met, I might have complied with your wishes, but it is not possible now for me to go back. I belong to a great nation that will do anything for anybody if asked; but, like you, we will never be driven, no matter what the odds," and I eyed his men and their muskets with a significant smile.

"What I now propose is that you send me under an armed escort to Khatmandu, where, if your Maharajah proscribes me, or does not sanction the perwana I hold from the Resident, then I promise to return with your guard, and you can deport me out of your country. Anyway, I assure you I will not allow the least blame to be attached to you by your superiors."

This speech had the desired effect on the mind of the Havildar, for with all his rough exterior he had in him the stuff that has made the Gurkha name famous in military annals.

He ordered his men to return to their quarters, told me I could proceed without interference, apologized for his rudeness, remarking that he was not accustomed to meet such a sahib, and that he should never forget me. This promise he and his subordinates well fulfilled some weeks later, when, on our return journey, they came out a mile or more to meet us, escorted us to their quarters, did everything possible for our comfort, while we put up in their midst for the night, and the next morning when bidding us a hearty goodbye, the old Havildar, acting as chief spokesman, came up with a smile that lit up his jagged features and said, "You are a sahib that will not require a perwana with us in the future."

EIGHTY-MILE GLACIER,
Descending 24 000 ft. till melted into a Foaming Torrent.

CHAPTER XII.

OUR FIRST VIEW OF KHATMANDU.

On arriving at the summit of the pass, we threw ourselves down to get some rest and waited for our servant to prepare breakfast. Harry was quite prostrated, but had been buoyed up by the excitement. The cold, crisp air, too, had the effect of a tonic, and we both at once became absorbed in a prospect not often presenting such extreme contrasts.

Eternal winter sat perched upon peaks confronting us, whose mantle of purity had never been defiled by the foot of man. Eternal summer reigned in the narrow valleys at our feet, variegated like patchwork with the different shades of crops raised in their little terraced fields in rotation by the frugal peasantry, whose small mud houses formed mere dots up the mountain sides. Far behind stretched the immense plain of upper Bengal which we had so wearily traversed, overhung with murkiness that was suggestive of a hot sun and ground radiating a fierce heat.

About us played the cool breezes wafted from the snows, singing after each other in and out of the fir tree tops when they would go to swell the grand chorus that came floating up at intervals from over the low lying ranges and out of valleys thousands of feet below us —a chorus formed by the combined hallelujahs of a multitude of silvery streams in their farewell descent from the "abodes of the blest."

Breakfast over and we at once began to descend, gratified to find that the path was not so steep as the one by which we had ascended to the top of the pass. Heavy overshadowing forests cut off all our view, though the peeps we got here and there revealed an almost perpendicular fall before us of some thousands of feet into a narrow, rugged gorge whose bottom was strewn with boulders and granite blocks, big as "double-storied houses." There they lay in the bed of a large stream, the Markhu, twisting and churning its waters into milky foam.

HIMALAYAN RATTAN SUSPENSION BRIDGE—FOR HOLDING ONE PERSON ONLY AT A TIME.

It was noon before we reached the bottom. Here the increased temperature made living almost unbearable. We passed through a small thatched village that lined the road and so near the bank of the Markhu that it must stand a good chance of being carried away in the monsoon. Beyond rose a high, rickety, wooden bridge over which our road was carried and at an elevation fully a hundred feet above the bed of the stream, showing what the constructor of the bridge thought of the possible rise of the river in a flood; and he was right, for 50 to 100 feet we found in such deep narrow valleys was not an unusual rise.

We did not care to mount this high, airy bridge, but passed through the bed of the stream upon a temporary structure of brush and stones so common in the Himalayas, thrown across streams during the fair weather months, with enough passages underneath to let the water flow through.

For the first time since leaving the Terai our road now began to be bordered with cultivated fields, small for want of room, but very fertile, with pretty little houses scattered about, surrounded by winter wheat, radishes and other growing cold weather crops—the pleasing beneficial results of thrift and patient husbandry. The country grew more thickly populated, the peasantry we found courteous and hospitable, and when Harry gave out completely, we were conducted to a shady veranda of a neat house beside the road and made comfortable.

After a long rest Harry awoke refreshed, partook of some broth and declared we should not stop on his account; so we again packed up and proceeded. We crossed and recrossed the Markhu several times by the fair season bridges, already described, came to the fine large Powah, also called Markhu like the stream, but being distant from any village it was not suited to us owing to the difficulty of procuring food supplies, so we pressed on having to make an abrupt ascent out of the Markhu valley of two to three thousand feet. This brought us to high open ground well cleared and cultivated, the houses of the peasantry astonishing us by running up to three, and even four and five stories, with their roofs covered by tiny flat tiles.

Just at dusk we entered the flourishing town of Chitlong, or Chota Nepal, some thirteen miles from Bhimphedi, and passed the night in a rectangular open building, bordering the road, but very much out of repair. Could we only have gone on another mile, we would have come to a very fine large Powah, but the darkness forbade this. We also learned that there were much better quarters inside the town, close to the place where we had put up, but we did not care to go there, it being as we found already occupied by a large noisy party belonging to some of the Nepal princes journeying down into India on the backs of seven elephants. How these monsters manage to go over such ground as we had traversed, and how they surmount the high passes, is a mystery, and must be seen to be believed and appreciated.

Our Chitlong night suddenly developed into a stormy one, the rain and mist being driven through our too freely ventilated building by violent gusts of wind. We managed, however, to keep dry and by morning the storm cleared, when the temperature as suddenly fell, producing cold that chilled us through and forced us to rise and move about to start up our circulation.

We were determined to make one forced march that day, and, if possible, reach Khatmandu by evening, the distance being only fifteen miles. However a high pass intervened which we would have to surmount, and this caused us some doubts. At all events we decided to make the attempt, and if Harry's fever, which had not returned since the past night, did not meanwhile come on again, we felt sure of covering the whole distance by night-fall.

Our progress at first was along a fair road slightly ascending between two spurs that met on the Chundragiri range, where, in a depression on the ridge and at a point 7,186 feet above sea level, was situated the Pass of the same name as the range over which we had to climb. After accomplishing two miles we began the steep ascent, and it was while tugging away to reach the top, that Harry's fever again set in, causing us grave doubts about getting through that day.

Half-way up we fell in with a string of coolies (they always like to travel in large companies) carrying cotton twist, cloth, Swedish matches, American kerosene, country soap, pig-iron and copper ware. What struck us as odd was that these coolies had themselves hired other coolies at Chitlong to help in carrying their loads for them up over the pass. One poor half-famished, gaunt-looking fellow told me he was carrying a bundle of saffron weighing over a hundred-weight, all the way from Benares to Khatmandu, some three hundred miles, and had been marching steadily twenty-seven days, receiving for such an undertaking the high inducement fee of seven rupees (or about ten shillings, equivalent to $2.40!) Out of this he was paying to have this load carried up the pass for him.

More than once we had occasion to notice the quantities of country soap made in small balls, sewed up in cloth bags, weighing up to two hundred pounds, that were brought from Mozufferpur and other neighboring Indian towns (where they were manufactured) into Nepal. The business must be a large one.

By 10 a. m., we reached the top of Chundra-giri (meaning the "Moon mountain") pass, and found the ground whitened by hail stones of the previous night's storm, and covered with hoar frost, though the sun was shining brightly. Our eyes were now treated to a recherché banquet covering such a stupendous spread, and composed of such innumerable courses that no pen of a ready writer or brush of a master painter could ever portray and do it justice. Chitlong and its valley lay on one side of us; on the other, and at a greater depth, stretching out east and west, was the valley of Nepal proper, twenty-five miles by ten. This valley is more like a plain, where no doubt once rose and fell the waters of a vast lake, before it had worn for itself the only outlet through the encircling chain of highest mountains, by what now marks the course of the Bagmati stream. This outlet once secured, the waters of the lake were drained off, leaving the bed to form the present fertile valley.

In its centre, plainly visible to our unaided sight, figured the houses, palaces, pagodas and temples of the capital city of Khatmandu, lo-

PANORAMA OF KHATMANDU, NEPAL'S CAPITAL.

cated between the two streams of Bagmati and Vishnumati. Close by and south of it extended another city, the old capital Patan, while far beyond, at the head ot the valley, appeared Bhatgaon, a still older capital. All about were thickly scattered farm houses, surrounded by extensive cultivations, and as if the level of the valley did not afford sufficient room for the crops, the fields were carried a long distance up the picturesque slopes that everywhere encircled the mountain sides. Above the fields extended the forests that soon belitttled themselves as they approached the abodes of snow and completely retired from the presence of a perfect sea of crowned heads culminating in that white-headed, grey-bearded monarch, old Everest, 29000 ft. high.

This monster, though a hundred miles off, was distinctly visible as his bifurcated cone-like head pierced the sky and formed the farthest point visible in a north-easterly direction, though we tried our best to penetrate the blue beyond and get a peep at our familiar Darjeeling friend, Kinchenjunga.

Finding this impossible, we ran our eye

along the towering heads and shoulders of the giants nearer to us, flashing their brilliants in the sunlight.

Fully one-third of the extensive visible horizon we found was required to give sufficient accommodation to this aged royal assembly. Out of their number the nearest to us were Gosain Than, 26,000 feet, Yassa, 24,000 feet, Matsiputra, 24,400, and Diwalgiri, 26,800. And as we looked up to them from our own lofty position in the grand stillness of that magnificent morning, we were inspired with awe at the sublime spectacle, and felt an inclination to uncover our heads; for they seemed to have penetrated into the very precincts of heaven and communed with the Invisible whose glories they reflected. What wonder that the Hindoo associates with each one of these tremendous peaks the abode of some of his deities, and thus has formed, clustered about him, a grander pantheon than the Greeks ever conceived of! The Himalayas (or the "abode of snow" as the name signifies) might more fittingly be termed the "Abode of the Infinite."

CHAPTER XIII.

WE ARRIVE AT THE NEPAL CAPITAL.

It was while our thoughts were thus absorbed in the grand panorama described in the previous chapter, when like one in Holy Writ we might have exclaimed "It is good for us to be here," that our coolies caught up with us and broke the spell, forcing us to descend to the coutemplation of common everyday affairs, as suddenly as they occasioned our descent some 2,500 feet, by a most abrupt, stony, precipitous, slippery, dangerous path to the village of Tankote. There we struck the level of the Nepal valley and sat down in the pleasant veranda of a neat farm house to partake of our last meal before going on to the city, still ten miles distant, though over a level, bridged, carriage-made road as we afterwards found. There to our surprise we met a Calcutta-built carriage (imported in sections) drawn by a couple of walers, (Australian bred horses).

Harry's fever had now left him though he had had quite a tussle with it, and while the attack was not quite so long as that of the previous day (perhaps from not giving away to it) yet it had left him weaker. While waiting for our lunch to be got ready, we had a look around and were particularly struck with the large number of trees and birds, as being the same we were accustomed to in Tropical India, but owing to Nepal's elevation above the sea (4,500 feet), they appeared somewhat modified, suggesting a compromise between the tropics and the temperate zone.

We were in the midst of our lunch when the mother of one of the Nepal queens passed by with two slave girls, all seated in a Howdah perched upon an elephant. There was quite a string of attendants, palankeens, dandies or sedan chairs, and coolies following. The Princess looked like an old lady of light complexion without the usual disfiguring Indian purdah or veil; she was apparently not strong, yet was bound for Holy Kasi (the Hindoo's name for Benares) on a pilgrimage, to bathe in the sanctifying stream, propitiate the deities with votive offerings to return with a quieted conscience and a cleaner soul. The Princess and her slaves descended from the elephant near us and entered palankeens, not daring to make the ascent of Chundragiri perched upon his lofty back. This emphasized the criticisms that we had made upon the policy of such a powerful and independent State as Nepal in keeping up its only direct communication with the outside world by a mere path for its highway.

It was evident that Nepal, from motives of supposed policy had done her best to utilize the barriers of nature for rendering access to her soil most difficult. This might have answered the requirements of by-gone times, but as the writer afterwards informed some of the Nepalese princes, such an out-of-date policy was now simply suicidal. The lack of easy communication was made specially aggravating at that time by the fact that the telegraph though brought to their borders was not allowed to be extended to their capital city.

I added that nature had evidently intended the most feasible course out from their valley to be viâ the Bagmati, and this would readily bring them into India, from which quarter they had nothing to fear and much to gain. For pledged as England was to be her ally, should ever an occasion arise for her to send troops into Nepal, she would not march them over the passes of Cisagurdi and Chundragiri, but her engineers would adopt a much easier route, simplified by nature like the one above indicated. Why, therefore, should they not also take advantage for themselves of a more available road, thereby enlarging trade, developing their revenues and building up a prosperous, enlightened State? But more of this afterwards.

It was now 3 p. m., so packing up for the last time, we started with our coolies and reached the city gate by sundown. We passed through narrow, filthy streets for a mile, then got out on the other side of the city, whence we were conducted into the limits of the British Residency grounds, and here in a small building set apart for travelers we found

THE BRITISH RESIDENCY—KHATMANDU.

grateful shelter and congratulated ourselves on having accomplished the distance of about one hundred miles from Segowli in a week without any serious mishap.

The following is a resumé of our itinerary showing hours of actual travel:

Darjeeling to Calcutta . . .	26 hours:	375	miles by railway.
Calcutta to Segowli	22 "	440	" " "
Segowli to Persowny	10 "	26	These distances were done by daily marches, mostly on foot, and give a total ot 102 miles accomplished in 8 days. The straight route to Khatmandu would give 96 miles but we preferred a slight detour to secure a better road.
Parsowny to Semrabassa .	8 "	10	
Semrabassa to Bechiakho	4 "	10	
Bechiakho to Hetowdad . .	5 "	12	
Hetowdah to Bhimphedi .	12 "	15	
Bhimphedi to Chitlong . .	13 "	14	
Chitlong to Khatmandu .	12 "	15	

The next morning we received a kind message from the Residency surgeon asking if we needed anything. I sent back "salams" (thanks) by the servant, saying we required nothing, and that I would call upon him by noon. The doctor and the Resident are the only Europeans dwelling in Nepal, and now that the latter was away, the doctor was doing duty for the Resident as well.

My call was a pleasant one. He invited me

to come over with Harry and put up with him. At first I hesitated, but the day following we went with all our impedimenta and were made very comfortable in his new double-storied brick house, with a pleasant garden, abounding in roses, and bordered on its westerly side by a grove of pine trees, beyond which the ground rapidly descended into low, swampy land laid out in rice fields—rice being the staple crop of the entire valley. A Gurkha lieutenant, deputed as the daily orderly officer from the Nepal Court to the Residency for carrying messages, now called on me at my request and conveyed to the Maharajah my wish to see him and pay him my respects. The term Maharajah, though meaning king, has the exceptional use in this State of being applied to designate the Prime Minister, while the king himself is called Maharaj-adhiraj, who in the present instance was a mere boy of ten years, not troubled much with State affairs. Our host was not very sanguine about the old Maharajah caring to see me, stating that he was a staunch Hindoo, with a strong antipathy to Europeans and

HIS MAJESTY NEPAL'S YOUNG KING.

THE RESIDENCY-DOCTOR'S HOUSE.

HOLY SWAYAMBHUNATHA SHRINE.

averse to having anything to do with them; certainly not an encouraging prospect. So when the orderly returned, I was not surprised to be informed that the Maharajah could not see me now but would be glad to meet me soon, which was only a polite, oriental way of saying next week, or next month, or never.

However, there was no alternative but to wait until the interview was granted, for without that indispensible formality, I could neither call on anybody nor attempt to transact any business, nor ask anyone to come and see me. Not knowing all about these rules I had tried to get word to a merchant (who by the way was a native of Bengal and hence a British subject) to come and talk with me on any business or other matters when possibly I could assist him. He returned an answer that he should like to very much, but that this was impossible until I had had my first audience with the Prime Minister; and more than that not till he himself had applied and obtained permission to meet me, which he declared would on no condition be allowed him till the Maharajah nad seen and talked with me!

Besides, it was hinted, that if I expected to do any business with the Nepalese I must on no account stay within the limits of the Residency grounds, for everyone who went or came thither incurred some degree of suspicion and was subject to strict surveillance from the Nepal officials, an ordeal no native willingly underwent.* This advice that I change my quarters was all very well, but was not so easily done as said, since no European on any account is allowed to live in the town or neighborhood; at least not till the Maharajah's express sanction has been obtained; and this I could not look for until after the oft-mentioned and anxiously expected audience.

So now there was nothing left for us to do but to fill up as best we could the intervening leisure hours. Fortunately I had brought along a camera and though able to secure only a few negative dry plates, which the past monsoon had badly damaged, we determined to put them to good use, and in this way to

* It is to be regretted that there is, socially speaking, no intercourse between the Residency and the members of the Nepal court or Durbar. So much suspicion might be allayed, so much espionage abolished, so much good effected by a pleasant friendship between the two parties.

TOP OF SWAYAMBHUNATHA HILL AND SHRINE.

occupy ourselves with what results my readers must judge. In this connection I would acknowledge my indebtedness to Mr. Hoffman, of the firm of Messrs. Johnson and Hoffman, photographers, Calcutta, for giving me a few dry plates, and also for the accompanying portraits of the Nepal Princes to illustrate my narrative.

Mr. Hoffman had come up from Calcutta with a European artist assistant, to photograph the carvings and other curiosities that were being collected under the supervision of of the Residency surgeon for the Indian and Colonial Exhibition to be held in London as well as to take what pictures he could of the Nepalese officers and their court. In this he was very successful and was well patronized as he richly deserved to be.

Our first photographing trip was up a hill infested with monkeys, and crowned with a most conspicuous gilded shrine of Swayambhunatha, about two miles towards the north of the Residency, outside the city walls. To reach it we had to pass over a badly paved road and when we got to the foot of the hill we came upon a broad flight of ancient stone steps numbering some three hundred and fifty, worn smooth by the feet of millions of devotees, and guarded at the bottom by a couple of large stone griffins together with a huge statue of Sakya Sinha or Buddha.

The steps grew steeper as one ascended and finally when the top was reached, three hundred feet above the base, a very fine view of the city and encircling snow-capped mountains was obtained. At the very entrance of the collection of shrines crowded together above is an immense brass thunderbolt of the god Indra, shaped like a huge hour-glass laid across a pedestal or platform three feet high and plated over with brass sheets covered with animals in bas-relief.

Just-back of this rises fifty feet high the solid rock of the top of the hill cut out into a colossal Bhuddistic dome or Chaitya, surmounting which there is a tapering wooden Pagoda, running up for another fifty feet, capped by a chutter or umbrella which reflects the sunlight from its gilded sides and is visible to the whole valley, reminding the traveler of the pagodas in Burmah raised by pious hands

SPECIMEN OF ELABORATE WOOD CARVING—KHATMANDU TEMPLE.

on every commanding point along the Irrawaddy.

This Chaitya formed the prominent centre around which a whole Pantheon of Hindoo deities in stone and brass, besides copper bells, Bhutea prayer-wheels, and the graves of the dead, were arranged with no apparent order, and we instinctively looked about expecting to find as well an altar dedicated to the Unknown God, for here at last was a spot where there was neither Jew nor Gentile, where beneath the shadows of the "Abodes of the Gods," the world's two greatest sects, forgetting their differences, had clasped hands; where Hindooism and Bhuddism had bound together in one volume their Sanscrit Shastras and the sayings of Sakya Muni, and where the Mongolian from Pekin with the Malabari from Ramyeshwar bent the knee side by side in the same sacred precincts consecrated alike to Bhudda and Siva—a striking prophetic illustration for those who believe in the great harmony that is to come.

But there was another phase to all this: The "shades of the ancestors," assuming the forms of the most cheeky monkeys the world ever saw, disported themselves about, making light of these hallowed scenes, defiling even the Holy of Holies, taunting the most devout pilgrim with winks, smirks and fiendish grimaces; then, as if this was all a good joke, they would add injury to insult by daring, on the sly, with sacrilegious paws to snatch away the votive offerings out of the very hands of the sin-stricken penitents, escape with their booty and impudently sit down to eat it at their leisure, perched up beside the nostrils of the gods themselves and wipe their whiskers on the divine heads! What was most surprising, no one seemed to take notice of them, or resent their conduct, and great was the astonishment manifested by the monkeys when we went at them for trying to upset our camera, and especially when one old, red faced blackguard, who must have once been a thorough scoundrel of a Hindoo, thought of appropriating our camera cloth!

We here saw and photographed the finest bit of elaborate wood carving forming the side of one of the temple buildings, (unfortunately damaged by age) that is to be found in Nepal, and that is saying a good deal.

THE SHRINES AND CREMATORIES OF PASHUPATI.

CHAPTER XIV.

STRANGE PHOTOGRAPHIC EXPERIENCES.

From Swayambhunatha or Symbhunath,) as it is called for short) we made our next photographic raid on the most sacred of all Nepal's shrines—Holy Pashupati—purely Hindoo, three miles to the east of Khatmandu city, crowded thick with temples, bathing and burning ghats; its rows of stone steps leading down to the Bagmati, covered with early morning bathers and devout worshipers, facing the sun and mumbling over their *munthra thunthras*.

Here, every February, come wending their way from the most distant cities of India a gathering of weary pilgrims, numbering as many as twenty-five thousand, and without waiting for any special movement of the waters, but for the moon to become full, they have a dip in the sanctifying Bagmati. Hither, too, the dead and dying are hurried and laid where their feet will be washed by the sacred stream, to ensure for the soul a safe and rapid transit into the realms of bliss, and this ceremony over, the body (sometimes even while the fluttering spirit is hesitating to wing its long flight) * is made over to the flames of the funeral pile. Here also we were told was a spot where the forlorn widow used to commit *suttee*, by casting herself upon the burning pyre of her dead husband. This rite, however, is now abolished, the last recorded instance being at the death of the previous Maharajah, when his favorite wife immolated herself on his burning body.

The location of Pashupati is most pictur-

* I am here reminded of an incident told me by the Residency Surgeon. The young wife of a well-to-do Hindoo was struck down by cholera. Our friend, the doctor, was called and he hastened to attend her. She rallied and bade fair to recover. What was his surprise to be told two or three days later that the woman was being carried at that very moment to the Pashupati burning ghat. He mounted his horse and rushed down to the place, there he found his poor patient still alive, but laid out so that her feet touched the flowing stream, while beside her the wood was being arranged and the cremation ceremonies were under way. The doctor expostulated with the husband and relatives, and urged them to desist at once from their murderous intentions, as the woman was not dead. They finally were prevailed upon to stay proceedings and to take the poor woman home, where she survived three days, and but for her rough treatment and attempt at premature cremation, she might have lived and recovered.

THE HOLY SILVER TEMPLE AT PASHUPATI.

esque, situated on one side of the Bagmati, where the stream flows through a gorge with precipitous banks, a hundred feet in height. On the bank opposite—covered with trees and commanding a full view of the sacred buildings—we focused our camera and took the accompanying views.

One amusing incident occurred while taking the holiest temple of all—Pashupatinatha—with its gilded pagoda top or chutter. This shrine is the principal one in Pashupati, and has silvered doors half way up the flight of steps leading from the Bagmati into its court-yard. We had just taken one view and were duplicating it, when one of the attending priests happened to look up, and not liking our unhallowed gaze, though he had no idea of what we were doing, slammed the two silvered doors together with great violence, in exhibition of his disgust. As we were much above him on the opposite bank, and could look over into the court-yard of the temple, the shutting of the doors in our face, as it were, was rather an improvement than otherwise, for it showed their rich construction to better advantage.

This temple is deemed so sacred that though there is a public thoroughfare on the opposite side from where we stood, no European is allowed to pass along that portion of the road adjacent to its outer wall and entrance.

It was while contemplating this varied scene and thinking what a power Hindooism must be to invest so inaccessible an out-of-the-way corner with such soul-enslaving sanctity, as to induce Baboos from Bengal, Ascetics from the Punjab, Brahmans from the Deccan to come to do *puja* (worship) so many hundreds of miles, in midwinter, at great personal sacrifice—I say it was while pondering over all this that the thought expressed at the beginning of this account was suggested for the particular benefit of any possible readers among my large circle of esteemed Hindoo friends who will best understand the force of this inquiry—why we, *Vilayati Bhurts* (freely rendered "of the foreign priestly Brahman caste" —that is, Caucasian) could not lay claim at Pashupati to *some* punya, as our merited share, having come so many times further than the farthest-traveled pilgrim there!

BHUDDIST PRIESTESS PREACHING BEFORE THE MONASTERY.

Another fresh morning we devoted to the interesting tope of Bodhnath, about two miles north-east of Pashupati, a purely Bhuddistic shrine, without any mixture of Hindooism.

It is an immense, artificially-prepared, white-washed chaitya of bricks and mortar, with long rows of circular steps or terraces, rising in diminishing circles, one above the other, to the height of fifty feet, where the top of the tope is reached. Out of that rises an equally tall wooden pillar, or Bhuddistic minaret, surmounted by a gilded, brazen chutter, the umbrella being fringed with little bells having long, flat tongues. These every passing breeze causes to tinkle forth prayers, which at that elevation, so much nearer heaven, getting the start, precede and help to give greater acceptance before the great throne to the petitions rising from the devotees themselves below, as they make their peregrinations around the circular base of the chaitya, some two hundred feet in diameter.

What is more, further to ensure divine hearing, the praying supplicants, as they walk their rounds, encircling over and over again this imposing tope, give twirls to the many prayer wheels (over a foot long and not half as broad) arranged in a double row in niches in the masonry of the chaitya, keeping time to their step by chanting over-and-over the simple, expressive prayer that has consoled millions, being the first words lisped by the infant, the last breathed forth by the dying:—"Om Mani Padmi hom"—O God, the Jewel in the Lotus. Amen!—or, O God, let me attain perfection, and obtain eternal bliss. Amen.

All around this Bhuddistic shrine is a double storied range of buildings with shops below and dwellings above, completely encircling the tope in a kind of courtyard. During winter this place is filled with hundreds of Bhuteas and Thibetians, who come in caràvans bringing skins, woolen stuffs, bricks of tea, musk and gold dust—some of these articles on their own backs, and the rest laden on ponies, mules, yakes and goats.

We picked up some curiosities here, such as ornaments for women, some elaborate ones set with turquoises.

I should have stated earlier, that whenever we ventured outside the Residency grounds, we were required, from motives of policy, to have an orderly, or Nepalese soldier precede us and to carry a sepoy of the Residency Guard with us, and thus attended we used to make our various trips, followed by a coolie bearing our camera.

That it was necessary to be thus always provided with such a guard of honor I now question, for we have only the pleasantest recollections of all our excursions, and received nothing but courtesy and kindness from prince and peasant.

Just as we were getting somewhat impatient at not hearing from the Maharajah and at his not appointing a day for our interview, word came through the orderly officer that His Excellency, General Runudip Sing, K. C. S. I. (Knight Commander of the Star of India) would be pleased to fix upon Tuesday in the following week to have me call. This would bring about our meeting on the thirteenth day from the date of our arrival, and was sooner than our fears had allowed us to expect, realizing how painfully slow a course affairs are allowed to take in the East.

The few intervening days were spent in going about the city and in visiting Balaji, a Hindoo shrine about a mile and a half north-west of the Residency, and to reach which, we passed along a well made road completely arched over by a fine avenue of willows. This road was the work of Sir Jung Bahadur, who had an excellent wooden bridge, resting on stout piles constructed for it, where it crossed the Vishnumati stream.

The deity that interested us most at Balaji was a huge recumbent figure of Siva, with an immense cobra de capello entwined about him, the whole resting on the petals of an open lotus flower—all cut out of solid rock—and made to appear as though floating on the surface of the water in the midst of a tank. Women were offering rice and flowers in connection with their morning devotions. There were a series of other tanks close by, built over the beds of springs and so constructed as to let the overflowing water pass off through figured stone spouts in graceful streams from one tank into another.

OUR MILITARY ESCORT ABOUT KHATMANDU.

The great attraction here were the hundreds of sacred fish large and small, very tame, and fed at Government expense.

As a background to Balaji rose the mountain of Nagarjun to a height of many thousand feet covered with thick forest. All around its base ran a masonry wall, extending over twelve miles, and built at great expense. It enclosed a vast game preserve where all kinds of animals were reared for affording the princes occasional sport. We were told that even golden pheasants and white peacocks brought at great expense from China were here turned loose with the hope of their thriving, but the venture proved a failure.

On the stone slabs surmounting the Balaji tanks we were shown reddish spots like blood stains, which the guard in charge of the place declared had rained down in the storm that overtook us the week previous at Chitlong, and which he in great earnestness assured us was a bad omen, portending an early calamity, and that the same had happened before in Nepal history with dreadful realization. We smiled incredulously, dismissed the remark from our thoughts and went on.

Our rambles in the city itself secured us some characteristic pictures, and much insight into Nepal daily life. One of the best general views obtained of the city buildings and lanes, was from the top of the Dharera a substantial masonry pillar, two hundred and fifty feet high, containing a winding staircase and built by General Bhimasena Thapa in 1856. It resembled a lighthouse in all but the light which it lacked.

Permission had to be obtained to ascend it, which was readily secured, and from its narrow masonry apertures we could look down on one side and see several thousand Gurkha soldiers going through various drill movements under officers dressed in English uniforms, who, in order to be consistent, shouted out their various commands in English, though none of the troops understood that language. The esplanade where the troops paraded was a splendid stretch of ground, all made and leveled at great expense, running close along the city wall and just outside of it. The troops are drilled here every day and with slight intermission, often from morning till

THE SACRED FLOWING TANKS AT BALAJI.

NEPAL'S KING AND HIS GENERALS.

GURKHA TROOPS PARADING BEFORE THE ROYAL TOWER.

GENERAL JIT JUNG.
(Late Commander-in-Chief.)

evening, and this seems to be the *one* great pastime of the nobility. No games or other manly exercises are at all popular with old or young, a fact to be regretted.

Nepal has a standing army of 15,000 men, drilled and armed with old muzzle-loading guns, and, in any emergency, could put into the field more than three times that number, of either time-expired men, or men who have some knowledge of soldiering. Indeed, every family has to contribute one of its male members at least as its quota to the military establishment, and to a stranger going about Khatmandu and neighborhood every other man he meets seems to be a soldier in dark blue uniform.

The bulk of the troops are infantry; there is no cavalry, unless a mounted guard be called such (they would be of little use), and only a small force of artillery. There are boy generals and gray-headed old lieutenants, the results of an autocratic government, where all power is held by one who cannot be questioned, and who deals out the honors to the nearest and dearest.

The maintenance of so great a standing army, out of all proportion to her ordinary needs, is Nepal's greatest mistake, and can do her nothing but harm. There seems to be a perfect craze among her nobility for the profession of arms and for no other; thus diverting a good share of the revenues and of the country's best brain and sinew from channels where they could be far better employed in building up the prosperity of the State and strengthening the lines of its independence; for, as already stated, Nepâl has nothing to fear from India, and with England as her sworn ally she has nothing to fear from Thibet.

As regards India, were Nepal from any insane cause to attempt to withstand her, all her own population, added to all her troops, could oppose no effectual resistance, and history already has shown that though she might fight Thibet alone successfully, yet Thibet, backed by China, is more than a match for her.

No, let Napal keep an army, but only a small one, and on the German plan let her educate, if she chooses, all her subjects in military tactics, so that when required, she can turn

NEWAR WOOD-CARVERS AT WORK.

into the field at a moment's notice a whole nation of drilled troops. One cannot help feeling at times that England is doing her best, by her bribes and presents of vast stands of arms and immense quantities of ammunition to the States on her frontiers, to induce them to keep up a ruinous standing army for no other purpose than to use them as a buffer against the growing spectre of Russian aggression towards India. If true, she has much to answer for, and much to suffer from her own gifts, should the buffers turn the muzzles the wrong way.

Nepal has made attempts to manufacture her own arms and ammunition, but the results have been very poor. That she does not take hold of this matter more intelligently and efficiently is inexplicable and inconsistent with her great fondness for the profession of arms.

But to go back and take up our camera left on top of the Dharera looking down on the parading Gurkhas: On the opposite side from the esplanade lay the capital city of 50,000 inhabitants wedged in between the

Bagmati and Vishnumati, extending up from the point where these streams unite, and presenting a most picturesque appearance outwardly, but inwardly reeking with filth; a city which has dunghills for its foundations, stagnant pools for ornamental lakes, whose streets do duty for drains and latrines, where the widest thoroughfares are narrow lanes wretchedly paved, only fit for inoculated pedestrians. Such is Khatmandu, with its ever present effluvia and stench, so that it is no wonder that during the summer just closing ten thousand, or one-fifth of its population had fallen victims to cholera.

Indeed the wonder is that they did not *all* die by that fell disease, about which I had the opportunity of telling the Maharajah that it was much more of a dangerous intruder than any European could be. I told him, moreover, that but for his making it so congenial for the loathsome monster to take up its residence in his Capital, it would never come. I added that he, the Prince, had it in his power, by a little attention to sanitation, to banish the wretch so that it should never

BLOOD-THIRSTY GOD BHAIRUB.

put foot in his dominions again, provided as His Excellency was by the Almighty with a climate that was fatal to this rabid pariah.

It was owing to this unhealthy, polluted state of the city that we disliked much to frequent the bazars, streets and shops, though each time we went we saw some new and exquisite carving, some temple or other object of interest that incited us to go again, and each time we returned we had a fit of nausea.

The carvings of Khatmandu are certainly the most elaborate and profuse of any to be found in the world. Not only are the temples and palaces covered with carvings, but even private dwellings, including often the doorways of the meanest hovels are loaded with a degree of ornamentation that is simply overwhelming.

There are peacocks with outspread tails, griffins, snakes, fruits and flowers, gods and goddesses, delicate lattice work, and screens to represent the most graceful artistic designs, looking at a distance like gossamer lace that might be marred by the slightest breeze.

These carvings, however, have one most objectionable feature, they are too often disfigured by the most outrageously obscene representations, the reason assigned for such gross exhibitions of indecency being some occult charm, or some mysterious, magical influence they have for warding off evil!

All carvings (except a few in stone) are made in the splendid sal wood brought up from the Terai forests and are the handiwork of a class of artisans who are paid but three or four pence (eight cents) a day, whose ranks are growing rapidly thin for want of encouragement and patronage, a fact that the Nepal Government should at once take note of and remedy before too late, seeing that the public taste is degenerating so that the present requirements are for a style of ornamentation that at the best is a poor class of painting, appearing on the buildings more like immense gaudy daubs than anything artistic.

The most hideous object we saw or photographed was an immense stone carved image of Bhairub, an unmistakable god of death that might well stand to personify cholera. This monster is dancing on a prostrate figure, and seems to be surrounded by an atmosphere of skulls. He stands close to the king's city palace, in the midst of the central bazar, and is built into a solid masonry wall, very near another important deity called Hanuman or the monkey god.

While picturing Bhairub, surrounded by an inquisitive crowd that almost crushed us and our camera in their eager curiosity, which we always did our best to gratify, we were thinking of another and more serious crowd that used to gather about this fiendish monster in years happily now past, when human victims were dragged into his presence and decapitated to satisfy his supposed blood-thirstiness and thereby stay the ravages of an epidemic, or ward off some impending public calamity!

Thanks to British influence, and to the late Sir Jung Bahadur's enlightened views, the god Bhairub has to content himself nowadays with the sacrifice of buffaloes and goats, whose heads and horns, according to the prevailing custom in Nepal, are nailed up so as to adorn the lintels and doors of the neighboring shrines. In all sacrifices the blood only is used about the deities while the flesh is taken away and eaten.

Close to where we fixed our camera was an enormous copper bell, suspended from four stone pillars standing on a high stone platform, that might claim twin-ship with the great one at the Kremlin in Moscow, and would do credit to any foundry of modern times. But it would be a tedious undertaking to describe all the objects that are here crowded together around the King's city palace, overtopped by the gilded and burnished tapering pagoda-temples, whose roofs of solid polished plates of brass and copper were dazzling in the sunlight the most noteworthy of all being Taleju, built by Raja Mahindra Malla, A. D. 1549. I therefore hasten to that feature of the bazar—its shops—that from business motives interested us.

We had to confess to being disappointed in these establishments. They were smaller and inferior to those in places of less importance in India. The goods, too, were of less variety. There were Manchester (England)

ENTRANCE TO KING'S CITY PALACE, KHATMANDU.

LAMA DOCTOR AND HIS *HOCUS POCUS.*

sheetings and prints, Birmingham cutlery and hardware of the cheaper, coarser sorts, and brimstone matches.

The country-made articles were few and of rough description, such as woolen and cotton cloth, brass and ironware, copper bells, and good, tough, indifferently-bleached paper, made by hand, in sheets not quite a yard square, out of the bark of a species of the Daphne.

Each sheet cost a cent, or halfpenny, and even if bought in quantities would not be much less. It equalled in strength our best parchment, was coarser and thicker, and was used by everybody, including the Government, for their correspondence, business records and official documents.

CHAPTER XV.

CURIOUS RACES AND SOCIAL CUSTOMS.

Of the people met in the streets each had to the practised eye his distinctive mark in dress, cast of features and language, showing the race to which he belonged.

There were Hindoos—and under this head may be reckoned first and foremost the dominant race of the Gurkhas—and the lower castes of Magars and Gurungs.

Next may be mentioned the Bhuddists—the Newars, Bhuteas, Limbus, Keratis, and Lep chas, and, if we except the Newars, all are a dirty, ugly lot, with very strong Mongolian type of features.

Last, and least, are the Mahomedans, composed of Cashmeri, Kabuli and Irani (Persian) traders, hardly numbering a thousand.

Of all the above named races, the most numerous are the Newars—a mild, industrious, good-natured people, the owners of the soil, before the Gurkhas invaded their rights and dispossessed them, a full century ago.

They are the chief traders, agriculturists and mechanics of Nepal. Their women strike a stranger as very religiously inclined, for they are to be seen on various days visiting Symbhunath and other shrines in crowds, equally believing in Bhuddism and Hindooism. They are quite light in complexion and of symmetrical features, while a pleasant custom prevailing among them (even to some extent among the men) is the wearing of roses and other flowers in their hair, which is always gathered up and tied into a long knot upon the top of their heads.

The women of the other classes wear it plaited down their backs, ending with a red tassel. All the women have more freedom than their northern India sisters, in that they are allowed to go in public without being closely veiled, though many wind a white sheet around them outside of their clothing, reaching from head to foot.

The best dressed people as a class are the

Gurkhas, of good regular features, but generally of diminutive stature, though wiry and strong. They do not take kindly to work of any sort, being essentially a military race. They claim to be Rajputs by descent, having been driven out of Rajputana, in Central India, by the great Mahomedan conquerors.

The Princes themselves trace their lineage directly back to the Royal house of Oodeypore. Their language is Parbatiya, a modern dialect of Sanscrit, and written in that character, while that of the Newars is quite another language, and written in a different character.

Polygamy is allowed and practised by the well-to-do, though a widow cannot remarry among the Gurkhas, while the Newars do not object. Early child-marriages are in vogue. While we were there the present little king, ten years of age, was having his nuptials arranged for, we were told, to one not much over half his years, and the marriage actually took place after we came away.

All the people seem to eat flesh of some kind, even that of buffalo and wild pig. In

NEPALESE WOMEN WEAVING.

this the Hindoos differ from their more southern brethren. It seems strange that although the buffalo could be killed and eaten, the very idea of *beef*, as we understand it, is perfectly abhorrent to them, and the killing of a cow is ranked as murder of the first degree, and punishable with death.

Among our instructions from the Residency, we were to give no offence in this respect, though this caution was quite unnecessary, as we had long ago learned the lesson to respect the religious prejudices of all nations. Rice is their staple diet. Of vegetables, too, they have a variety, and are particularly fond of radishes fermented by exposure to the sun. Thus prepared, the stuff keeps for a long time, and is called Sinki, though it might more appropriately bear another name similar in sound, on account of its searching and offensive odor.

The lower classes drink a liquor which they distill from rice, called Rakshi. The upper classes are forbidden this indulgence, on pain of losing caste. Notwithstanding all injunctions to the contrary, the traffic in imported spirits—English brandy, French wines and the like—pays well, showing that somebody takes kindly to intoxicating beverages, caste or no caste. It seems a thousand pities that the influence of the white man tends to increase the drinking habits of all natives with whom he comes in contact. It is a well-known fact that the youthful members of the Gurkha nobility, who are sent down to Calcutta for their education under European masters, return victims to the craze for the strongest foreign liquors, imported brandy being their chief drink.

Tea drinking is very popular with all who can pay for the luxury, the tea used being imported in pressed bricks, brought all the way by caravans from China *via* Thibet. Here is a market for which the India tea merchant might compete.

Education and schools are not yet estimated at their full value, but there is a growing demand for them, and the Nepal Government has more than one Baboo from the Calcutta University to take charge of quite a large school (in a fine long brick building facing the parade ground), composed chiefly of young princes and children of the upper classes.

Every scrap of available ground in the valley of Nepal is cultivated to exhaustion, being put under heavy contribution to yield its utmost to support a population already too large for its limited area to sustain.

Even the mountain sides are called upon to contribute a share, by having the fields carried in terraces some distance upwards towards the summit, as already observed.

There are, to be sure, half a dozen other valleys among the adjacent mountains, which afford valuable assistance, and send in a good share of their products to the city, but they are all small, the largest being Noakot, and as it is lower than Nepal, it produces, on account of its higher temperature, the fruits raised in India. Its oranges are excellent, grown on the banks of the Trisul Gunga, which flows through the bottom of the valley, and lower down bears the name Gunduk. No European is allowed to cross this stream.

I might mention here that the elevation of the Nepal valley is estimated at 4,500 feet above sea level, with an average annual rainfall of 55 inches. The thermometer falls only now and then in winter as low as twelve degrees below the freezing point; and rarely exceeds, in the hottest season, 80° Fahrenheit. Thus the winters are mild and the summers never uncomfortably hot.

Owing to the scarcity of land, every field is made to yield two and three crops a year, consisting chiefly of rice, wheat, Indian corn, radishes, garlics, potatoes and red pepper. A spot was pointed out to us where cardamom (*Alpinia cardamomum*) also was raised. The place is half a dozen miles to the south of the city, where through the religious zeal of some Hindoos getting the better of their judgment they had in memory of Nasick and Trimbuck, places of sanctity down near Bombay, located there a fresh source of the great Godavery river, close to which were several large flourishing gardens of cardamoms, the property of the State and which yielded the Government considerable revenue.

The general method of preparing the soil in Nepal is of the most rudimentary kind, and though the farmers believe in enriching their fields by a regular system of manuring we noticed that tillage was limited to digging the ground by hand with pickaxes—very rarely did they make use of ploughs, which are of the most primitive kind.

Seeing the Nepal valley is thus taxed to its utmost by the unceasing rotation of crops, flocks and herds are scarce. Poultry, however, is reared in large quantities, in which connection the great pains taken with the raising of ducks amused and interested us. Every morning the peasantry in their trips to their fields would carry their quacking families, distributed in baskets suspended from the ends of a bamboo resting on the shoulders of either man or woman. On reaching their feeding grounds they would let them out to pasture, and at evening drive them back into the baskets, often with a good deal of trouble and delay—a sight that caused us many a laugh —and then swinging the pole across their shoulders, which provoked a most noisy chattering among the fowls, they trudged home with them!

Slavery exists in Nepal. The number of people thus held in bondage we were told falls not far short of 30,000, though we doubt the accuracy of so high an estimate. All well-to-do families possess slaves,and the highest classes own great numbers of both sexes. They seem to be exclusively used for domestic work. Most of the slaves are such by descent, their forefathers having been so for generations. They are not imported from any other country, while their ranks are augmented at times by fresh additions from free families, who are brought into servitude as a punishment for misdeeds and political crimes.

Women slaves sell for Rs. 150 to Rs. 250 or £12 to £20 ($100), men slaves for a little less. Any slave having a child by her master can have her freedom. Both sexes are treated leniently, and with consideration, rendering them content with their bondage,

This whole system, however, has a most demoralizing effect on account of the women slaves and their debasement.

For a counteracting influence, as supposed by

A NEPAL PRINCESS AND HER SLAVE GIRLS.

LAMA OR BHUDDIST PRIEST AT HIS DEVOTIONS.

some, each family has its own *guru* or Brahmin priest, like a private chaplain. This office is hereditary; at the same time there are thousands of this priestly profession idling about the city attached to this or that deity, fed at the expense of the State and given free quarters.

I conversed at some length with one of this sanctimonious class in his own language—Mahrathi—to his great surprise. He came from a village near Satara of the Bombay Presidency and tramped as a bairagi—religious mendicant—from shrine to shrine, covering a distance of 3,000 miles in two years. By that time he had reached this sacred spot, where he meant to end his days, clothed by public charity and fed from the Government bounty.

In addition to the *bona fide* priests, a number assuming their garb, and in other ways religiously disguised as Bhikshus, etc., find shelter here from the outside world, even though they may be suspected or are real criminal characters, fleeing from impending justice, and unless the Nepal Government is asked to search for this or that particular one, all such find an asylum here and no questions asked.

This was particularly the case with numbers during the Indian mutiny in 1857, when among the fugitives came also the Nana of Bithdur—Nana Sahib, of odious fame—having made clean his escape to the Terai forests. He did not get further, however, as he was overtaken by a deadlier foe than the British rifle, and was hastened by the ghastly jungle fever to his still more ghastly account. This was stated to us as a fact by General Kadar Nur Singh, and hence the failure ever to find a trace of the rebel chief in spite of the handsome bounty placed on his head. His widow lived in a large comfortable house, pointed out to us, close to Sir Jung Bahadur's palace, and was allowed a monthly stipend by the Nepal State until she died in 1886.

The head of all this large religious community is the Raj Guru, or Archbishop, a very wealthy, influential man, possessor of immense estates, and of a liberal income from the State. He lives in princely style and wears the most costly jewels. We met him more than once driving out in a fine two-horse English-built carriage, with many attendants.

Thus, with the spiritual wants of the people looked after, their physical weaknesses are attended to by a class called Waids (or Waidya—doctors), proficient in native drugs; but there is no public hospital, nor a place for dispensing medicines to the people. To this I should make the exception of the good work done by the Residency surgeon, who has been constant in doing his best to make up for this sad want, while he spared no efforts and incurred much danger by his exposures during the recent severe cholera epidemic laboring in order to mitigate its ravages.

He has a neat little hospital in the rear of his house, where the sick are daily treated, among whom we noticed many afflicted with the disfiguring complaint, so prevalent in the Himalayas, of *goitre* (hideous swellings on the neck). Others we saw were principally Bhuteas, who had come miles from over the Himalayas to be vaccinated, having suffered fearfully from the scourge of small-pox. These had great faith in being inoculated—a belief not so well shared in by the other Eastern classes to their own hurt.

Justice is fairly administered, while the very severe and cruel punishments in vogue years ago are now abolished. There is no undue waste of time over technicalities, no exasperating formalities, no expensive fees, no disagreeing juries, and no devouring lawyers. The case is stated, the decision given, the decree executed. Capital punishment is resorted to only in cases of murder, rebellion, treason and the like, while women and Brahmins are degraded and imprisoned for life, these being the extreme penalties of the law for them.

Cases of conjugal infidelity, happily not frequent, are treated by the Newars lightly, but the Gurkhas punish such conduct very severely.

The Maharajah is virtually the Chief Justice and the head of the Nepal Court, and to his decision are referred all important cases by the magisterial judges, who, however, in all other minor matters, take affairs into their own hands. The laws of primogeniture prevail in Nepal as they do in India.

NARAYEN HITTI OR KING'S PALACE AND RAJ GURU'S TEMPLE.

The one thousand and one taxes. which eat into the vitals of more enlightened States, are quite unknown here. Every family pays to the Government, as their share of the land revenue to be collected, one-half of the produce they raise. With the other half they are able to supply all their few wants and to live a life of contentment.

After this divergence, occupying no more time, however, than we spent in our interesting lofty perch at the top of the Dharera, above the smells and noxious gases of the streets, we will return to point out just two more objects—Thapathali and Narayen Hitti; the former the extensive palace of the late Sir Jung Bahadur, and the latter the palace, or rather collection of palaces, of the King, Prime Minister and Raj Guru.

Both palaces are outside of the city walls; the first named is located near the apex formed by the junction of the Bagmati and Vishnumati; the other in quite the opposite direction, between the Residency and parade ground. The latter is much too crowded, and on account of its hemmed-in location does not show to any advantage, though some of the buildings are five and six stories high, while Thapathali is better situated and makes an imposing appearance.

It used to contain, in the days of its late enlightened lord, four large public rooms thrown open to visitors, where was an exceedingly interesting collection of Chinese, Thibetian and Nepalese curiosities, together with a unique and varied assortment of shikar (hunting) trophies, all arranged alongside of European articles, from chandeliers and pianos to mechanical toys and chromo-lithographs.

None of the above palaces, though ranking first in importance at Khatmandu, have any of the fine quaint carvings showing the deteriorated taste of the present age, which make so many of the older structures, even of the commonest sort, so pleasing and interesting; and what is worse, these royal structures are great rambling brick buildings—without any pretense to architectural beauty, covered entirely with whitewash, which but for the cleanly appearance, outrages one's feelings.

One great improvement that could be readily

THAPATHALI—PALACE OF THE LATE SIR JUNG BAHADUR.

undertaken, and which would contribute much towards beautifying and making attractive the above palaces, would be the construction of fountains (they have nothing of the kind), fed by water brought easily from a neighboring stream.

This water could at the same time be utilized for drinking purposes, and, if distributed in aqueducts over the city, would at once displace the contaminated stuff drunk by the people from the polluted city wells and from the equally polluted streams, at once lessening the death rate.

CHAPTER XVI.

IMPRESSIVE INTERVIEW WITH THE MAHARAJAH.

But our time is up, and we must hasten to 12 o'clock breakfast at our kind host's, the doctor's, and after that get ready for the interview appointed with the Maharajah for that afternoon.

It was suggested that the Maharajah would send a horse or conveyance for me, but I sent word to decline this, as the doctor wanted to see the Maharajah himself on some business and offered very kindly to take me with him in the Resident's carriage. On the way the doctor warned me not to be too sanguine about the interview, adding that the Maharajah, after the first formalities, might say only a few words, and that ten minutes would be as much time as he would care to allow for our call.

We went through two or three gateways,

GENERAL RUNUDIP SING.
The Assassinated Prime Minister.

passing sentries with drawn swords and loaded muskets at each, and then came to the palace entrance proper, though there was nothing to indicate this especially. Here we dismounted, went through a room curtained off, and entered an open court, perhaps a hundred feet each way, around which the palace had been built several stories high in the form of a square. This court contained only a few plants. Walking across to the other side we were at once ushered into the large audience hall fitted up with English furniture, chandeliers, paintings and European ornaments.

Here, surrounded by quite a staff of brightly uniformed officials, all decked out in brilliants and with rich plumed turbans and helmets sat the Maharajah, General Runudip Singh. He at once rose, came forward, pleasantly shook hands (his were encased in white French kid gloves) and asked us to take seats, one on either side of him.

The officers arranged themselves in chairs in a semicircle on each side of us. He looked like a man of sixty with a decided will of his own; sharp eyes and a firm lip, but to judge from all accounts not at all equal to his brother, the late Sir Jung Bahadur, in abilities or liberal ideas. He was not in uniform as his officers were, but in a plain suit of English pattern, the coat buttoning up to the top, patent-leather boots, and a fine rich cap.

He asked me about the journey up, how I liked his country, and finally my object in coming. I replied to all these inquiries to his apparent satisfaction. I should have preferred speaking only in Hindoostani as the Prime Minister understood that language and afterwards we did converse together in this manner, but at first I was obliged to speak in English (not a word of which the prince understood) while his nephew, a most intelligent man, General Khudgo Sham Shere Jung, educated at the Doveton College, Calcutta, interpreted to his uncle.

Instead of the doctor's ten minutes interview, the old Maharajah seemed to warm up the more he plied me with questions, until dispensing with interpreters and resorting directly to Hindoostani himself he kept me busy talking for nearly an hour.

He showed me a most profusely carved bedstead inlaid with tusks, artificial eyes, and worked up into elaborate designs, and wanted to know if the mechanics of England or America could turn out such an article as that. I replied I did not think they would have the patience to keep working at one bedstead for a couple of years—an answer that greatly amused him. He then showed me hunting trophies, and finally took me to a large, life-sized painting, hanging on the wall, of the Burra Maharani (great queen) the first of his two wives.

I had with me at the time a copy or two of the "Scientific American" and of the "American Exporter." These the prince asked to look over and seemed very much interested in so large and varied an assortment of illustrations; one thing that especially pleased his fancy was a large drawing of some fine cows—the "Holstein-Friesian Cattle"—such cows as that he said were worth having, and wished me to arrange at once to get out a few for him!

At the close of our call I asked for leave to go about, and visit his officials and the merchants, and that they be permitted to see me. This was no sooner asked than granted. I then intimated the hope of seeing him again soon, as I wished to talk with him further about business, and about certain improvements that I would like to propose; such as the introduction of pure water into the city, etc. In response to this he gladly gave me permission to call again and discuss the projects suggested.

I little dreamed then what an awful calamity awaited him within a week from that time, and that I should never see him again.

Our interview ended with the usual "*pan supari*," or betel-nut—seed of the areca palm done up with catechu, cloves, cardamoms and wet lime in a narcotic leaf of the Piper Betel, whose folds are pinned together by a clove, and the whole wrapped up in silver foil and made just large enough to go into the mouth. This was further supplemented by the pulling out of handkerchiefs and the dropping on them of a little attar of roses, oftener rose water simply and not attar.

Feeling encouraged by the pleasant impression I had received of the Maharajah, I went about making acquaintances in the city at the same time that I was planning to obtain another day when I should call again on the prince by royal permission.

Here it occurs to me to say, how often and often has the thought come up, in my many wanderings into the remote unfrequented Eastern corners of the earth, what a grand field these places would afford to so many of our energetic, adventurous spirits for stretching their limbs, aching from ennui, and for airing their cramped feelings.

They could gratify their love of Natural History or fondness for excitement and the chase, instead of pining away at their homes, or in luxurious enervating hotels, for something novel, for something out of the worn threadbare routes of travel, tourists' resorts and fashionable watering places. For want of a little information and better employment, these idlers fritter away their superfluous time as well as their superfluous cash in wasteful ignorance and chafing monotony, who could do good and get good by coming out to the East. I should be only too glad to assist any such, wishing to make a trial, with information and the results of my experience, assuring them that many of these trips would cost less than the sums frivolously spent in a few weeks at Brighton or Saratoga.

It was during this time while going around Khatmandu that I became greatly interested in reading about Bogle and Manning's trips into Thibet, and what difficulties they encountered in their efforts to reach its capital, Lhassa (said to be three months' journey from Nepal where there is a large Nepalese colony), all of which is narrated in a most instructive and entertaining book edited by Clements Markham, which was kindly lent me from the Residency library.

This book presents in unfavorable comparison the present apathy, if not positive hostility, of the India Government, as exhibited through their Foreign Office, towards all private commercial efforts for opening up connections with the frontier countries.

If there was one thing above others that reflected the greatest credit on India's first Viceroy, the Marquis of Hastings, it was this: he took a deep personal interest in all efforts to extend friendly feeling and develop trade dealings with the far north, beyond the confines of British possessions.

It will never be known what the Eastern world and England lost by the sudden death of that most excellent man, the Grand Lama, head and autocrat of all Buddhism in far-off Pekin, after months of terrible journeying from his revered city of Lhassa, intensified by the strange coincident of the equally sudden death at Calcutta of Bogle, the emissary of the Marquis, on the eve of both these noble representatives' contemplated conference with the Emperor of China in Pekin itself, for the promotion of commercial and friendly reciprocity.

CHAPTER XVI.

THE MAHARAJAH'S ASSASSINATION.

It was while I was reading these intensely interesting narratives of Bogle and Manning, mentioned in the previous chapter, and while seated with the Doctor around a wood fire in his drawing-room late one Monday evening, that the Jemadar, or head of the Residency body guard, consisting of eighty sepoys—native soldiers of India—came rushing in unceremoniously and whispered audibly: "Hulla hai!!—there is a massacre—going on in the city—there is a massacre—going on in the city!"

We looked up incredulously; at which he seemed additionally excited, and asked us to come outside. We followed.

The night was perfect, bright with a full moon; but a startling phenomenon at once riveted our sight. The whole heavens seemed to be streaked with the trails of showers of in-

A NEPALESE PRINCESS.

cessant shooting stars (noticed all over India and elsewhere, being the annual November meteoric display), presaging some great evil according to the superstitious, while below from the direction of the city, arose the ominous low din of some great confusion, and the tramp as of bodies of troops in motion.

Then came the sharp, piercing *réveillé* of the bugle, followed by the rattle of musketry and the deep booming of cannon. There were sounds of people running hither and thither, shrieks from women, and a great uproar generally. All came upon us like a thunderbolt out of a cloudless sky, and no one could solve the mystery.

The scenes of violence, passion and cruelty enacted that night pass all telling, and although the doctor hastened off spies to find out the meaning of such commotion, yet long before they returned, our pleasant, quiet quarters had become a house of refuge for those who had a few minutes before been reckoned among the highest in the land, resplendent in gems and finery, and whose very nod was sufficient to call whole regiments into action.

Among the first to come was General Kadar Nur Singh. I had met him at my interview with the Maharajah, dressed in full, rich uniform; now he was barely covered with a thin suit of under garments, as he rushed up breathless and entreated to be sheltered from impending death. Close on his heels came General Dhoje Nur Singh, the adopted son of the Maharajah, and his little boy with him. They were in a sad plight and were not at first recognized, being woefully changed from their appearance as last seen at the palace decked in royal robes and ablaze with precious stones. Then came in hot haste the brothers, General Padum Jung and General Rungbir Jung, sons of the late General Jung Bahadur. Last of all, after many hair-breadth's escapes, came one of the Queens, the second wife of the Maharajah, called Jetta Maharani,* seated astride a little saddle fastened upon the back of one of her slave girls (as is customary among all Nepal ladies of rank, for they are much averse to walking even in their houses).

* Another Rani called "Chitti Biddi My" was detected just before she reached the Residency limits, and ruthlessly carried back and put into rigorous confinement.

These, with their followers, took up a good portion of the Doctor's house, and each one had harrowing stories to tell, while one and all confirmed the report of the Maharajah's assassination in his own palace, as he was reclining, looking over official documents. In addition to this they reported other deaths and claimed that but for the security granted them under the shadow of the British flag they would have been made away with by a cruel faction, simply to further the end of a political party.

Thus, in a few words, is portrayed what had been only a repetition of Nepal's previous history over and over again; for either the King or Prime Minister had come into power by violence and bloodshed, or been deposed and brought to an untimely end by the same desperate, cruel practices.*

We now recalled the rain of blood drops shown us at Balaji, and realized with what ineffaceable conviction this and the falling stars that night would be henceforth associ-

* The eldest son of Sir Jung Bahadur, General Jugat Jung, his wife and son were the principal persons killed next to the Maharajah, and their bodies were carried down unceremoniously to Pashupati and hastily cremated.

ated in the minds of the Nepalese with the troubles just happening!

The doctor sent off at once a special messenger to recall the Resident, although it would be nearly a week before he could get back, while we noticing an apparently quieter state prevailing out of doors, retired to secure some sleep as best we could.

The next morning there was all about us a close cordon of Nepalese guards, stationed outside the Residency limits. The city seemed to be completely under martial law. The shops were closed, the streets were as silent as death and the fields about were deserted by the peasantry.

Our plans were now all thrown into confusion and we hardly knew what was best to be done. Of course we felt free to walk out, and did so, but we could see no one, and as the doctor thought we were rash and made light of the situation, we stopped going around not wishing to give offense to anyone, least of all to our kind host.

A rather long week for us went by. Meanwhile negotiations had been begun for de-

GENERAL JUGAT JUNG AND WIFE.
(Killed in the Massacre.)

porting down into India the refugees, who were still with us. The Resident, too, had arrived and we, taking advantage of the lull in the political horizon, ventured out on two or three short trips. One was to the old capital of Patan, close by, which we found to be a cleaner city, which is not saying much; and containing many beautiful temples. One of stone was particularly fine, situated with a number of others highly carved in the central square.

We also made an excursion to the oldest capital of all, Bhatgaon, built by Raja Anand Malla, A. D. 865, where the streets are wider, better paved and cleaner still, than in either Patan or Khatmandu, though the town is of about the same size as Patan, numbering perhaps 35,000. Here the carvings, taken as a whole, were the finest, and those on the oldest buildings seemed to be the best.

The old palace was especially handsome and had in front of it a tall monolith crowned with the brazen figure of the Rajah who built it. We found these monoliths in many places elsewhere, surmounted with some long-ago defunct hero or mythological winged being called a Garud. These figures are put in a kneeling posture, generally facing some temple, and have a bell-shaped umbrella over them, or a brazen snake coiled around them with its head extended upward and made to overhang the figure. On the snake there sits usually a little bird.

But the temple that interested us most at Bhatgaon was the five-storied temple of Nyatpola Dewal. None but the priests ever enters it. Its long flight of stone steps leading up to the masonry platform on which the temple proper rests, are lined with figures as shown in the illustration. The lowest steps are guarded by two powerful giants, Jayamalla and Phalta, peylwans or champion wrestlers of the Bhatgaon Court, and said to be each stronger than the combined strength of ten men. Above them are placed two elephants, each stronger than ten of these men. Above them are two lions ten times stronger than the elephants. Then came two Sarduls or griffins, as much stronger again, and fifth and last, above all, comes two goddesses of super-

PATAN SHRINES.

NYATPOLA—BHATGAON'S HOLIEST SHRINE.

PALACE AT BHATGAON.

natural power called by the euphonious names of Byaghrini and Singhrini.

From Bhatgaon we went up to a place of pilgrimage called Mahadeo Pookri, and here had a grand view of mount Everest, across a sea of valleys about eighty miles off, the nearest point from which Europeans as yet have gazed upon that giant. Owing to the great distance, Everest is somewhat disappointing, being not nearly so striking and impressive as several nearer peaks.

The following account taken from the Bombay *Gazette* describes a Frenchman's recent experience and ideas of Nepal.

A FRENCH ARCHÆOLOGIST IN INDIA.

This is the fourth letter published under the signature of "Gustave le Bon," in *Le Temps*:—

Gulf of Bengal, on board the S.S. Sir John Lawrence.

I find myself returned from the mysterious capital of Nepal, which no other Frenchman had yet visited, and, in spite of all the pessimist predictions with which I was loaded, I have preserved my head upon my shoulders without very serious difficulty.

It is, as everybody knows, only under very exceptional circumstances that a European—English or not—is able to obtain authority to visit Khatmandu and the principal towns of Nepal; but then, even when this authority has been obtained, it does not necessarily follow that all difficulties are removed. To undertake to cross the Himalayas in four days, the 170 kilometres which separate the last English town, Motihari from Khatmandu, one must have—at least a vigor, and a familiarity with mountains which no member of our Alpine clubs certainly possesses—and a small army of porters. Part of the road is done in a sort of palanquin which in shape is exactly like a cradle. It is as ugly as it is uncomfortable. The reflections one makes during the forty-eight hours you spend in this box are only disturbed by the cold baths you inevitably receive in your clothes every time it is necessary to cross the course of a stream. Arrived at the foot of the Himalayas you are squeezed into a sort of bag called a dandy—I know not absolutely why—carried by four men, by means of crossed poles, and if your porters chance only to slip once—no one hears more said of you or them—otherwise you arrive all right at Khatamandu.

In the temporary absence of the English authorities at Motihari, I had to recruit—with the aid of a certain very dangerous and expensive native magistrate of the name of Elphinstone—thirty-three porters who constituted certainly the most remarkable collection of rascals that I have ever had occasion to see in my travels. Thc band had looted my bag of rupees, and would even have wished to seize everything if they hadn't first exposed themselves to make acquaintance with the bullets of my revolvers. Their trick, the most ingenious, was to abandon mc for a whole night in an extremely dense forest, and dangerous after sunset on account of tigers, leopards, panthers, boars, and savage elephants, which swarm there, as rabbits in a European warren. Had I been devoured, and nothing more to account for my disappearance, they would have cleared themselves by attributing the accident to chance, and looted the rupees.

Unfortunately for them the protection of the gods baffled these perfidious attempts. The wood being too damp for me to be able by means of it to make a fire and disperse and frighten the ferocious beasts, I had recourse to candles, which had never quitted me, and, placed one upon the covering of the apparatus mentioned above, I then wrote, in order to keep me awake, a little work which I had thought of for some time, and which I have sent to the *Révue Scientifique* on a new method of taking observations *en voyage*, and upon the instruments that I would employ for this purpose, When the day appeared, one of the men of the gang, who had taken shelter in a neighboring village, came to see if the tigers had dined on European cutlets. I imagine it must have proved a very disagreeable disillusion when, instead of the bag of rupees which he expected to carry away, he found himself seized by the throat, and felt the barrel of a revolver introduce itself into his eye with an injunction to bring back the rest of the band within five minutes under pain of having his skull fractured. The band returned, a few strokes with a walking stick applied vigorously among the lot, with a threat of the revolver upon the first man who would speak a word, was sufficient to inspire a salutary fear in all these worthy friends. These little incidents of a journey to

Nepal, when one has not the English authorities to assist you at Motihari, are largely compensated for by the sight of the very curious town of Khatmandu, and, above all, that of Patan and Bhatgaon. I have already told you of the impression produced upon me by the temples at Ellora; those that I experienced on entering Patan were even a great deal stronger. The temples of Ellora recall more or less definitely to the traveler who has seen India, some things already known. The great royal palace of Patan or that of Bhatgaon represents, on the contrary, forms quite unexpected. There is in these two towns, on a surface of a few hundred metres, a collection of temples, palaces, and columns, such as might raise the dreams of the most fastidious of artists to an ecstacy. We see there, temples having the form of immense pyramids, superimposed, the vertices below, placed on the summit of gigantic steps, which one might almost believe had been cut by giants, covered with monsters, statues, gates of bronze and gold, guarded by a legion of fantastic beings. At the first sight of these strange marvels, one passes the hand across the forehead to know if he is not dreaming. I do not know in any other portion of the world among the works of men anything so marvellously picturesque. If the details of this striking effect are analyzed, you see clearly that the architecture of Nepal is formed by the combination of elements borrowed from the two countries between which it is situated—India and China. The combination of these two elements, so different, produces some effects absolutely unexpected. Certain columns have a formation which we would not be able to include in a classification

PUBLIC SQUARE AND TEMPLE AT PATAN.

BHATGAON TEMPLES.

of any of those known to us ; the same with the windows of the houses and their framing. Certain bronze doors of the temples or palaces of Nepal are of very remarkable workmanship ; but this work is a small thing in comparison with that of the wooden columns which generally support the first story of the houses. As to form, I know nothing in the world more superb, and as to work, the most skillful of Parisian artists would be certainly incapable of doing better.

The architecture of Nepal is but little known in Europe, and in India only by some photographs due to a photographer that the Sovereign made to come from Calcutta to his court to execute his portrait and those of his family; but these photographs, on a small scale, do not allow of the details of these monuments being seen, which are precisely the most essential parts, and only give in reality a very vague idea.

The arrival of a Frenchman in Nepal had greatly agitated the inhabitants, and during my sojourn, I had absolutely the pleasure of passing in the condition of a strange beast, such as a calf with two heads or a bearded woman. When I made my photographs and took my measurements I had over 2,000 persons round me or perched upon the roofs of the houses, entirely engaged in observing me. The two soldiers of the guard of the sovereign who accompanied me made way by distributing to left and right vigorous showers of blows with a baton, but the crowd would not resign themselves to go away even for a few steps. I finished by paying no attention to this mass of valorous people, wno only manifested any concern for me by curiosity without the slightest mark of hostility. This curiosity appeared to have spread, besides, to all classes of society among the people of Nepal, and to judge by the number of personages that the chance—it is always wise to attribute to chance the events of which we are ignorant of the causes—brought about me. In order to avoid hurting the susceptibilities of the English Ambassador—the only European authorized to reside at Nepal—I had carefully avoided paying a visit to the Emperor or any of his generals.

But most of them placed themselves in my way, and, besides, asked me most graciously the same question. The affairs of China greatly interest the inhabitants of Nepal. who have had many times to defend themselves against the armies of the Celestial Empire. Everyone knew that there was in the West, a great country called France, the Raja of which was at war with China. It was therefore evident that, if a Frenchman came to Nepal it was to determine the Nepalese Government to declare war with China, and thus gain a useful diversion. To essay to prove to an inhabitant of Nepal that a European could wish to come from so distant countries and encounter the difficult passes of the Himalayas merely to visit theit mountains is completely impossible.

The geographical situation of Nepal, which ought to be considered as a large valley situated among the highest mountains of the world, has always been dependent on her two redoubtable neighbors—the English of India and the Chinese of Thibet. It has valiantly defended its independence in many battles, and all that England has been able to obtain after a bloody war has been the authorization of having an ambassador at Khatmandu. Except this Ambassador and his doctor no European has the right to penetrate to the towns of Nepal without the formal authority of the Nepalese Government, and this authorization is only very exceptionally accorded. The English Ambassador himself is only allowed to travel in a very limited area, and the greatest portion of Nepal is rigorously interdicted to him.

In spite of its isolation, Nepal knows perfectly all that takes place in the world. The rich lords have their sons at the Calcutta University, where they learn to speak English, carry eyeglass and jacket. The eyeglass and jacket are quite exceptional in the suite of the Emperor. A happy chance brought the young Sovereign in my way; it embraced also his suite and all the ladies of his court. He was dressed in a violet mantle and his servitors had over their heads the insignia of the royal power, a parasol. The ladies followed in palanquins or hammocks covered with red silk disposed in a manner so as entirely to conceal their faces. There was not one, nevertheless, who passed with her head quite concealed, but looked to see what this stranger was like, who had been intriguing in the country for some time. Fine fellows, the Nepalese of the Imperial family, in spite of the evident mixture of yellow blood, and the marks which they paint upon their forehead. Few of the inhabitants of Nepal are able to boast of their good looks.

My letter is already very long, and I have spoken but little about the inhabitants of Nepal. I will return to the subject in a future correspondence, if the vessel which carries me arrives safely in port. It contains five hundred Hindus, who have saved pice by pice for a long time the sum necessary to make a pilgrimage to this celebrated temple of Juggernath, where, unfortunately for them, they are no longer permitted to be crushed under the car of their idol. This interdiction alone seems to throw a gloom over their happiness. Let us not sneer at them too much. Nowhere else in India does man risk his life for a chimera so vain as that of the idols of the temple of Juggernath.

The political atmosphere being now a little cleared, we began seriously to think about getting back to India, but wished before doing so to pay our farewell respects to the new *regime*, consisting of General Bhir Sham Shere Jung for new Maharajah, and his brother, General Khudgo Sham Shaw Jung, as Commander-in-Chief. There were a few other changes made, and positions filled, but so far as the little king was concerned, he was in no way affected by the disturbance, and was conducted about the city on an elephant just after the assassinations to show the people that their Rajah was all right.

The new Prime Minister appointed a time for me to call at the city palace, and I had a

NEPAL'S PRIME MINISTER, GENERAL BIR SHAM SHERE JUNG.

pleasant chat with him there, and with his brother, General Khudgo Sham Shaw Jung. The latter will be remembered as the one who kindly interpreted for me, and whom I have already described in my interview with the late Maharajah. He is a very energetic, affable and enterprising officer. He is the moving spirit in the new Government, and to him the Maharajah, though older, defers. Under these two brothers' influence the Nepal Durbar, or Court, bids fair to adopt improvements and introduce reforms that will benefit the State.

To my several suggestions as to matters most important to take hold of first, they listened with a spirit of approval, but told me that owing to the troubles they had just passed through, and to the necessity of giving their undivided attention to important State questions, they could not undertake anything of the nature I proposed, until they had made themselves secure in their new positions—an answer that admitted of no argument. However, at the special request of General Khudgo Sham Shaw Jung and his brother, I agreed to make personally a survey of what would be a feasible project for the city water-works, and placed the results of my estimate in their hands, with their promise not to let the matter sleep.

Feeling now that should any good come of our trip to Nepal, even if it had not profited us in any business way, the thought of having at least possibly benefited the State in some incidental way should console us for what we had undergone; and seeing that nothing further could be definitely accomplished in the present excitement and uncertainty that prevailed, we took our leave of the Maharajah and his brother with pleasant assurances of friendship, since repeated in letters.

In closing this chapter it may be well to refer to the old adage that history repeats itself, and with special rapidity in Nepal. General Khudgo Sham Shaw Jung, the new commander-in-chief, and who was the mainstay of his brother, the new Maharajah, and the principal factor in putting the old Maharajah, his uncle, out of the way, was himself obliged to flee the country not many months later in

GENERAL KHUDGO SHAM SHERE JUNG.
(Brother of Prime Minister.)

order to save his own head endangered by the jealous suspicions of his brother, General Bhir Sham Shere Jung, whom he had been instrumental in making Maharajah.

CHAPTER XVII.

RETURNING TO CALCUTTA.

After bidding the Princes and many native friends we had made good-bye, we, with many regrets, bade farewell to our most hospitable host the Doctor, and esteemed friend the Resident, and I take this opportunity to state that more kindly-disposed officials in all the circle of those among whom I have been forced to cast my lot I have failed to find.

I wish I could say the same of certain others who, though representatives of the India Foreign Office in different places visited by the writer, were anything but a credit to that department; who belied their professions and positions, who assumed most haughty, overbearing airs, who might well be asked, "I say, stranger, are you anybody in particular?" who

CORONATION OF MAHARAJAH GENERAL BIR SHAM SHERE JUNG.

used the prerogatives of their office to thwart you, whether traveler, sportsman, scientist * or commercial agent, who were as disgusting in their attempts to bully all those within their reach, as they were obsequious toadies to anybody with a title; who felt as uneasy at your presence as they were jealous of your success.

These men, though engaged on a generous salary to represent a great, liberal, civilizing commercial nation, might well be supposed to be the under-paid hirelings of an exclusive despotism; whose knowledge of the world and its requirements were as contracted as they were ridiculous; who were as wanting in brain, as they were deficient in the attributes of a gentleman; who were as lacking in their sympathy with the natives they governed, as in their knowledge of the language of the country they ruled; who thought they saw a Russian spy in every traveling foreigner

* We met a gentleman just after our return to Calcutta, who, as the representative of a scientific society in Europe, had laid all his plans to go over a good portion of the ground we had traversed. He communicated with the authorities and managed after many weeks' waiting to get their permission. On the strength of this he started, but was suddenly stopped on the border and the permission arbitrarily revoked. He of course had no alternative but to retrace his steps.

though a fellow countryman; when they could not distinguish a Brahmin from an Afghan nor a palm tree from a pine.*

In this connection I am reminded of an

---

* The following is an extract from the *Bombay Gazette:*

"Lord Roseberry was the principal speaker at a recent banquet to the Indians and Colonials by the Edinburgh Corporation. In proposing the toast of 'Our Colonial and Indian Empire' he welcomed the visitors to Scotland, and expressed pleasure that the colonists should make themselves acquainted with the great historic centres of the Empire. If (he continued) I were a legislator, a despotic legislator, such as legislators have been, and I had to frame laws for this great Empire, one of the first that I should frame would be this, that neither in Great Britain, nor in India, nor in the colonies should any man hold high and important office without knowing something of the Empire with which he was called upon to deal. (Cheers) I would make men who wish to be British Ministers travel in the colonies and in India (cheers), and I would make those who desire to hold office, to hold high office in the colonies and in India, see something of the islands from which so much of their inspiration at any rate is derived. (Cheers.) We used, in former days, not so very long ago, to have government by test in all its departments. There was a test for every office. It was. I think, a faulty test, because it dealt with conscience, and that is not a fair test; but I should be willing to re-enact government by test, for it is to test whether men knew those great countries, those vast regions, with which every man is called upon to deal. (Cheers.) I have done some part of that work myself, and I hope that it will not be long—indeed, a short time—before I visit that Indian Empire, which to all of us must be supremely interesting (cheers), as including not merely great historic memories which adorn and strengthen the character of this nation, but as containing a vast majority of the subjects of the British Empire, and as representing so considerable a key to our foreign policy, and moreover, as representing a great acquisition—an Empire within an Empire, which we are determined to maintain, whatever force may be arrayed against us. (Cheers.) We know something of those forces; we learn something of them every day; and it is for us in these days to show that the character of the nation which conquered India has not deteriorated, and that it is determined, in spite of whatever may happen, to maintain it."

official* who was stationed at Bagdad; he was a poor specimen of an Englishman and a still poorer consular officer who did not understand

* The story of this official reminds us very forcibly of some lines of Rudyard Kipling touching a similar character.

STUDY OF AN ELEVATION, IN INDIAN INK.

This ditty is a string of lies,
But—how the deuce did Gubbins rise.

Potiphar Gubbins, C. E.,
Stands at the top of the tree,
And I muse in my bed on the reasons that led
To the hoisting of Potiphar G.

Potiphar Gubbins, C. E.,
Is seven years junior to me;
Each bridge that he makes he either buckles or breaks,
And his work is as rough as he.

Potiphar Gubbins, C. E.,
Is coarse as a chimpanzee,
And I can't understand why you gave him your hand,
Lovely Mehitabel Lee.

Potiphar Gubbins, C. E.,
Is dear to the Powers that Be,
For they bow and they smile in an affable style,
Which is seldom accorded to me.

Potiphar Gubbins, C. E.,
Is certain as certain can be,
Of a highly-paid post which is claimed by a host
Of Seniors—including me.

Careless and lazy is he,
Greatly inferior to me;
What is the spell that you manage so well,
Commonplace Potiphar G.?

Lovely Mehitabel Lee,
Let me inquire of thee,
Should I have riz to what Potiphar is,
Had'st thou been mated to me?

what travelers and commercial agents or "tradespeople," as he stigmatized them, wanted to be "nosing about for," and if he could manage it, would have them all sent back from his territory. He used the State funds placed in his hands, not as they were intended, for entertaining, and bringing all foreigners in the town together into pleasant social intercourse, but to gratify a selfish, morbid taste for getting up private dinners and parties that cost him but little, in the interests of a select few; claiming that the rest, even though his own English country-men, were low class and unfit for his immaculate society. He was too great a coward to face you openly with his pitiable puerility, at the same time much too politic to overstep the bounds of his office so as to afford you a handle whereby you could criminate him. Yet his actions showed that he was not only foolishly officious, but at the same time silly enough to suspect that every stranger was the "everlasting Russian spy." Not only this, but he was in the habit of traducing the stranger, even if his own countryman, and of making it as uncomfortable for him as possible. Imagine such a being selected for an important office on the Indian Frontier, as for example to represent Her Gracious Imperial Majesty Queen Victoria in lovely Cashmere! Better have ten Russian spies "nosing about" than such a timid and apprehensive individual for a Resident in that happy valley just being thrown open to civilization.*

* We extract the following from a leading Bombay paper: —"The *Indian Witness* tells us that a gentleman who holds a Professor's chair in one of the Universities in the Southern States, has achieved a very unenviable notoriety in America, for refusing to shake hands with a gentleman of darker color than his own. He has very properly been removed from his appointment, his conduct having awakened great indignation. But two or three days before we saw this incident in the *Witness*, a gentleman, who was making a casual call upon us, in referring to the Resident at ——, told us with what indignation he had seen this gentleman openly insult a very distinguished native officer at the —— Court in the same way. The native gentleman in question held almost the highest official position in the native State. He is a man of refinement and education, and bears an unsullied character. Accustomed to meet Englishmen on a footing of courteous equality, he held out his hand to welcome the new Resident, in the ordinary way of shaking hands, not dreaming that it would be refused, and held it out long enough to create embarrassment. Our civilian Resident stiffly inclined his head, and refused to see the Minister's outstretched hand, and the latter withdrew it. If Lord Dufferin would like to know the name of this Resident and of the gentleman he thus insulted, we will give both. This same Resident, we are assured, in spite of the large allowances attached to his office, lives absolutely and entirely at the expense of the Court to which he is accredited as our representative. Not only his horses, but his table, his servants (we think) and the whole of his expenses, are paid by the Maharajah, with that diffuse hospitality that characterizes Eastern Courts. And the vulgar fellow who is not above receiving and profiting by this hospitality, is too great a man to show the ordinary courtesy of a gentleman, to the highest officer in the State, a man more than equal to himself, in all probability, in education and ability. We have no doubt that if we were to

Does the Anglo-Indian wonder he has a bad name? Is the English Government at a loss to know why it does not succeed better with its civilizing schemes and social reforms; why there is not more harmony between the governing classes and the governed; why there is not more in common between the officials and their own countrymen in India * even when the latter are wielding the most civilizing, harmonizing, reforming influences through the ramifications of business and commerce?

England's Indian frontier to-day would have been a wall of adamant against Russian ag-

ask this gentleman the cause of his rudeness, he would tell us that the *prestige* of his position required to be upheld by him. The Duke and Duchess of Connaught both shook the hand of this native gentleman warmly, as they did the hand of every official presented to them. But then a Royal Duke cares nothing for his *prestige*, and the civilian does.

"It may be questioned, we admit frankly, whether it is wise to notice such conduct or to let it pass. We confess that it is strong indignation only that leads us to notice it. The native gentleman to whom this insult was offered, is a distinguished graduate of one of our Universities, a man of high character also and of very great abilities. Our own feeling in presence of such conduct is so strong, that upon satisfactory proof that the insult was really offered, we should require this Civilian Resident to make his choice between an adequate apology to the gentleman he had insulted, and retirement from the public service. Under any circumstances, we should remove him from the political line altogether, a career for which he is plainly unfitted."

* It is well known that the last Viceroy of India, Lord Ripon, came very near being ingloriously "summoned to his account" through the murderous hands of enraged fellow countrymen who whether as commercial men in Calcutta or as planters of Darjeeling and Behar execrated his very name.

gression, had she from the first encouraged her merchants to establish business houses, with their many connections and agencies, throughout that misguided territory, inducing the natives and interesting their governments to apply their misdirected zeal and to invest their misspent capital in good roads and profitable branches of trade which would have enlightened, improved and fraternized this now incongruous fermenting mass of humanity.

Despite all the obstructions and the persistent efforts of these incompetent officials, who represent the Foreign Office, to smother the spread of commerce, some trade at least manages to percolate through the Indian boundary limits, if the following recent official report can be relied upon:

"Colonel Lockhart's Mission while in Gilgit, Chitral, and even further north in Wakhan, found that Manchester cotton goods had complete command of the market. Of course, the market was a limited one, for the country is sparsely inhabited, and the people are poor. English cotton goods had penetrated to these remote and obscure regions, were well known to the people and commanded a ready and growing sale. In Gilgit the average value of cotton appears to have been five yards to the rupee. Russian cotton seemed to be unknown, and what was not obtained from English sources was supplied locally or from Chinese Kashgar. A curiosity in trade was discovered in the fact that American firearms imported by way of Russian Turkestan were underselling English weapons brought from India. Thus a good revolver which had come all the way from Cincinnati, U. S. A., was purchased in Chitral for Rs. 15. The people think these arms are of Russian manufacture, but the factory stamp discloses their true origin."—*Extract from the "Bombay Gazette."*

I will not weary my readers with the details of our journey back to Calcutta. I will simply say that we did not encounter any difficulty, and got over the ground more rapidly than when coming—thanks to the Doctor and his fast horses, besides two Bhutea ponies lent us by the Nepal Durbar.

The first day's march brought us to Cisagurdi, where, as stated, our old friend the Havildar did everything for our comfort; the next day brought us to Hetowda, and the next to Bechakho. The following day being overtaken by a drenching rain in the gloomy Terai forest, which wet us to the skin, we found shelter in a hut beyond Semrabassa, having for a good share of its roof a thriving pumpkin vine. This place we carpeted with rice straw, and here we passed the night, feeling as comfortable as a prince in his palace.

On the following day we reached the pleasant bungalow of an Indigo planter at Ruck soul, just inside of British territory, and were freely offered every hospitality, even his well-stocked stable being placed at our disposal.

That same night we pushed on and reached Segowli Railway Station, expecting to make ourselves comfortable there with our bedding sent on ahead by the kind forethought of our planter host. In this, however, we were doomed to disappointment, as our coolies had concluded to ensure for themselves first a good night's rest somewhere on the road, no matter what became of us, and did not turn up till noon of the following day!

We had therefore to arrange ourselves on some chairs in the railway waiting-room. The night proved far too cold for our ordinary light clothing, so we placed lanterns under our chairs and spread over us several large newspapers, as wraps, thereby securing enough warmth from our improvised stove and paper covering to weather the night through fairly well.

It was pleasant to hear again the screech of the engine, the rattle of the car wheels, and to feel ourselves being whirled along behind steam once more. And thus it was while being borne back to India's capital, seated in a comfortable railway carriage that we had time to go over the different incidents of our eventful journey and came to the conclusion, in accordance with the thought suggested at the outset of this narrative that all travel had not yet lost its romance.

On our arrival at Calcutta * we were con-

* The following appeared in one of the Calcutta dailies the day after Mr. Ballantine's arrival in that city: "We learn that Mr. Henry Ballantine, the enterprising traveler and explorer, has just arrived at Calcutta, from Nepal. As he was the only European at the British Residency in Khatmandu, apart from the Residency Surgeon, who was an eye-witness of the troubl s consequent on the murder of the Maharajah and certain officials there, we fancy he could, if he chose, 'a tale unfold.' Probably the proper Government officials here already have had an interview with him, but, however that may be, we learn on good authority that Mr. Ballantine has be n commissioned by the new Durbar to make out an estimate for certain improvements for immediate execution. If these be really carried out, we can assure the new *regime* that no stronger proof could be given to the outside world and to the Indian Government of their good intentions and of their sincere resolve to institute a reform in that benighted corner of the earth, notorious for generations past for its habitations of cruelty. We congratulate Nepal in committing to such an enterprising gentleman any contemplated reforms; for in such good hands, they may rest assured of as great success as their wretched

gratulated by friends as if returning from an endeavor to discover "the Northwest Passage" or from looking up traces of the "Franklin Expedition," and the questions asked were a de- deplorable commentary on the ignorance of the capital of India about its important next-door neighbor.

---

city now stands deplorably in need of; while we could point Nepal to Japan and its present prosperous, independent and highly creditable stand among civilized nations, as a position worthy and possible of their attainment."—[*The Publishers.*]

THE END.

INDEX.

A

B

P

Q

R

S

T

W

Y